UNDERSTANDING
The Old Testament

H. L. Ellison, B.A., B.D.

Joshua, Judges, Ruth, 1 and 2 Samuel

D1634342

A BIBLE STUDY BOOK

Published in Great Britain by
Scripture Union
47 Marylebone Lane, London W1 6AX

INTRODUCTION

Since their introduction, Scripture Union Bible Study Books have enjoyed wide popularity both in their original paperback and more recently as the hardback Daily Bible Commentary. The continued demand has led to their production in this new format. They are unique in that they can be used both as a daily Bible reading aid and as a complete commentary on the Old Testament.

A Daily Bible Reading Aid

Each volume is divided into sections of an appropriate length for daily use. Normally each volume provides material for one quarter's use, the exceptions being 1 Kings — Job (six months) Proverbs — Isaiah (six months) and Psalms (four months). Sections have not been dated but where it has been felt appropriate that two be read together in order to complete the book within a quarter they are marked with an asterisk.

A complete commentary of the Old Testament

Every major passage is expounded with devotional warmth, clear explanations and relevance to daily life. Most commentaries follow the rather artificial verse divisions, but here the writers have been commissioned to divide the material according to the best exegetical pattern. They thus follow natural units which allow the comments to follow more closely the flow of the original writers thought.

Writers have generally based their comments on the R.S.V. and readers will probably find this is the most suitable translation to use, although the comments will be found equally helpful with any other version.

Joshua

Joshua, like the other books treated in this volume, and numerous others in the O.T., is anonymous. It is wiser and more reverent to accept this fact than to try to find an author. It is also unnecessary to ask when it took its present form, for the matter in it is very old, often contemporary with the events described.

It is not a history of the Conquest, but falls into three clearly distinct sections:

(*i*) The mighty acts of God during the Conquest (chs. **1—12**);

(*ii*) The fulfilment of God's promise (chs. **13—22**);

(*iii*) A warning for the future (chs. **23, 24**).

Joshua 1

Joshua's appointment as Moses' successor is recorded in Num. **27.18—23** (Deut. **34.9**); the reasons behind it will be found in Ex. **17.8—13**; **24.13**; **32.17**; **33.11**; Num. **14.6—10**.

Although Joshua knew that the conquest of Canaan could not begin until Moses was taken, his death was a heavy blow. There is a double call to courage: physical, as the military leader (6); and moral, in the keeping of the Law (7). God's giving waits on our readiness to accept (3); He never gives us blessings merely to be stored away in a spiritual bank waiting till we think we need them.

A careful study of the times involved in ch. **2** will show that the chapter must be fitted in after **1.10**—this is not unusual in Hebrew historical writing. The "three days" (11) are counted from the spies' return. Note the balance between God's guidance and human wisdom. Joshua was to enjoy special guidance (**5.13—15**, *etc.*), but he had also to acquaint himself with as much Scripture as then existed (7,8). The same principle holds good for us, except that as there is more Scripture for general guidance, we are likely to get less special guidance.

Palestine is not a country where military operations were possible the year round. We are not to think of the two-and-a-half tribes as separated completely from their families for six years or more; see

14.7,10 (just under 39 years elapsed between Kadesh Barnea and the crossing of the Jordan). There will have been "home leave" for some outside the campaigning season, while a flow of young men will have replaced the ageing, killed and wounded. The answer of the two-and-a-half tribes illustrates the principle that the true leader must always be out ahead of those he leads. From these tribes themselves we learn that God has no favourites. If we ask for special favours, we shall find that we are expected to pay a special price for them (*cf*. Num. 32). They were also to learn too late that their unwise material asking brought spiritual loss.

"Moses the servant of the Lord" (1): "servant" means "slave". This is the same title of honour as borne by the prophets (Amos 3.7), Paul (Rom. 1.1, *etc*.), and our Lord (Isa. 52.13, *etc*.).

Joshua 2

It was as right and proper for Joshua to send his spies as it had been for Moses earlier (Num. 13.1,2, Deut. 1.22,23). Normally God does not want us to be ignorant of what we have to face. The young men were betrayed, not by clothes or language, but by a certain freedom of bearing peculiar to the desert-dweller. Rahab was certainly a religious prostitute attached to the sanctuary, and as such a person of standing. The suggestion that she was an innkeeper comes from a deliberate false etymology given by the rabbis to the word translated "harlot" to save her honour. In going to her house the spies hoped to escape notice and to enjoy a measure of religious sanctuary. The king had to ask Rahab to hand them over (3).

Fear is a two-edged weapon, which we should use with care. It caused Rahab, who had obviously recognized who the men must be, to try and win the favour of their God by befriending them. It drove the others in Jericho to an even more stubborn resistance.

In vs. 15—21 we have a kind of story-telling common in the O.T. (The whole chapter is an example of it.) Clearly Rahab did not carry on a long conversation (16,21) in a loud whisper after the spies were already on the ground at the foot of the walls. We are first told of what she did (the important thing), and only then of the guarantee given her.

The "scarlet cord" (18) was not the rope used to let them down; that would have been far too conspicuous. It will have been only just visible to the keen-eyed Israelites below, while awakening no suspicion among the townsmen. The spies could give no unconditional guarantee to Rahab and her family. No sign attached to their clothes would have been sufficient to protect them in the excitement and hurly-burly of the capture of Jericho. They had to be protected by the easily identifiable house as Noah and his family were by the ark.

When Prof. Garstang excavated the ruins of an earlier Jericho, thinking they were Joshua's city, he found that part of the wall remained standing when most collapsed. The same probably happened to the section with Rahab's house (*cf.* **6.20,22**). Its high position prevented its roof from being overlooked (6).

How many people recognize us as Christians when they see us?

Joshua 3.1—4.18

The story carries straight on from **1.10,11**. Old Jerusalem is just about 2,500 feet above sea level; Jericho and Shittim about 850 feet below. From Jericho the floor of the Jordan valley slopes gradually downward for about six miles and then drops steeply about 150 feet to the trench (here 1,200 feet below sea level) about a mile wide through which the Jordan flows (the Dead Sea is 1,285 feet below). The trench is filled with jungle growth through which the river twists like an inebriated snake. It was not the river so much as the jungle that was difficult to cross, the fords of Jordan (**2.7**) being as much ways through the jungle as across the river. In spring the flooding of the Jordan (**3.15**) fills the trench, so they had a raging torrent, in places nearly a mile wide, between them and Jericho. Two agile young men might cross, but not the women, children, and cattle.

By the collapse of the banks the river was blocked at Adam (**3.16**), sixteen miles to the north. This happened to our knowledge in A.D. 1267, 1906, and 1927, with people crossing dryshod. The miraculous was not in the means but in God's complete control of Nature, so that it happened, not by chance but at the exact moment God willed it.

The gap between the ark and the people (**3.4**) was designed to impress on the people that this was entirely God's doing. It needs no explaining why the circle of stones was set up in Gilgal (**4.20**), but what of the circle in the river itself? If faith failed and scepticism laughed at the miracle, God could always dam the river again and let men see the hidden stones. There needs to be a sure memorial to God's salvation, hidden from men, in our hearts, to which we can look when men deny the reality of God's power.

The Levitical priests (**3.3**). The death of Nadab and Abihu (Lev. **10.1,2**) cut down the number of legitimate priests available. When local sanctuaries multiplied after the Conquest, there were not enough priests, and some accepted the task without God's call or sanction. The story is at pains to stress that only legitimate priests had the right to carry the ark.

What form does the danger of outrunning the ark of God take in Christian experience?

Joshua 4.19—5.15

Israel's last night in Egypt was the fifteenth of the first month. Now, forty years later, all but a couple of days, the purpose of the Exodus was accomplished (4.19). Canaan as a type is explained in Heb. 4.9,10; it is not a picture of heaven, but of that stage in the Christian life where we have learnt that it is not our effort but Christ's power that matters.

The dismay of the kings of Canaan (5.1) must apply even more strongly to Jericho. As the people moved down from Shittim (3.1) they must have been seen from the walls of Jericho. Doubtless before the miracle happened the west bank was lined by soldiers from Jericho. They must have fled in terror as they saw the water disappearing. That would be why they made no attempt to molest Israel in the next few days.

The command to make flint knives (5.2) was probably intended to stress the entirely new beginning. Nothing they had brought across Jordan should be used for the purpose. The command for a second circumcision, which, taken literally, would be impossible, presumably means that the rite would now have a deeper meaning than when it had been commanded to Abraham (Gen. 17.9—14). *Then* it was a pledge of a promise; *now* of a fulfilment. Life in the wilderness must have been very difficult and strenuous, so the neglect of circumcision can be understood. The "rolling away of the reproach of Egypt" lay in their new position as free men with a home. As long as they were in the wilderness they had not achieved the purpose of the Exodus.

Passover coincided with the barley harvest (11; *cf.* Lev. 23.9—14 with v. 15, which shows that the sheaf was brought in Passover week). The "old corn" rightly disappears in R.S.V. (11). The manna ceased when it was no longer needed. Special provision by God can be a sign of immaturity rather than of special spirituality.

Joshua's vision (5.13—15) is to be compared to Moses' (Exod. 3.2—5). It was his divine commissioning for his task. The purpose of the vision was not to give Joshua any special instructions—these he received, presumably through the high priest, whenever it was necessary—but to create a reverent attitude of heart and mind. We

6

can easily become more interested in special guidance than in a right relationship with the Guide.

Thought: Obey Rom. **12.**1,2, *and you will have guidance when you need it.*

Joshua 6

We find one reason for God's long delay in giving Canaan to the Israelites in Gen. **15.**16. "The iniquity of the Amorites" was the misuse of sex in the name of religion, which acted as a moral poison inside and outside Palestine. Before He punished them, God gave them ample time for repentance. Now He was bringing in Israel as His executioner. That the behaviour of v. 21 was not normal for Israel is shown by Deut. **20.**10—18. In addition the case of Rahab (23) shows that any Canaanite could have saved his life by sincerely accepting God's will and repudiating his past.

The Conquest mostly followed normal methods, but it had to start with a ceremony that would reveal its true nature. The presence of the Ark, not normally taken into battle, the silent ranks of armed men, until the shout of victory was raised (16,20), and the solemn blowing of the rams' horns, all stressed that this was a solemn religious ceremony. Then the destroying of all that could be destroyed, and the handing over of the remainder to God (19,24) went beyond the normal to show that they were not common plunderers but emissaries of God's judgment.

The marching ceremony was not very long, once the few miles from Gilgal had been covered. They could easily march round Jericho, while keeping out of bowshot from the walls, in twenty minutes. How gruesome to the inhabitants of Jericho the final two hours and more of silent marching with the wailing of the rams' horns must have been! The fall of the walls, like the crossing of Jordan, was probably due to God's supernatural use of the natural. The Exodus had been marked by considerable earthquake activity (Exod. **19.**18, Judg. **5.**4, Hab. **3.**6, Psa. **114.**4), which may have so weakened the walls that they were more ready to collapse when the time came.

It was God's purpose that Jericho, probably the oldest continuously inhabited settlement in Palestine (as shown by Miss Kenyon's excavations) should remain a ruin for ever as a token of His judgment on the past; this did not include the neighbouring groves of palm trees (*cf*. Deut. **34.**3, Judg. **1.**16, 3.13). For the fate of the man who defied the curse see 1 Kings **16.**34.

If God's punishments are to be understood by those He punishes and their contemporaries, He must act according to standards they understand. For the man of Joshua's time, when a thing was devoted, or put in the ban (*cherem*; so 6.18,19, 7.1), it had a curse on it which demanded its destruction. Anyone taking devoted articles into his house or tent automatically brought the curse on it and all in it. Achan's family was not killed as an extra punishment on Achan but because they had come under the curse, as had the cattle and the tent (24). If we think such a punishment unfair, we must not forget that Achan knew the penalty of his action; if God had acted otherwise, he and others would have thought that God had condoned the act of rebellion.

Joshua's self-confidence (4) was not the cause of the defeat, but if he had asked God first, he would have discovered the sin without the defeat. The despair of Joshua and the people was due not to the size of the defeat but to its unexpectedness. The clearly implied rebuke in v. 10 is due to Joshua's assumption that God was at fault. He should have realized that the fault must be Israel's, even though he could not know the exact reason. Joshua's preoccupation with God's great name was, of course, mainly a preoccupation with his own safety.

Spare a thought for Achan's agony as he witnessed the choice of the lot drawing inexorably nearer to him (16—18). Joshua says, "Tell the truth" (19a); by acknowledging that the result of the lot was correct, Achan would give glory and praise to God.

The Valley of Achor is one of the deep, dark ravines that cut into the mountain backbone of Palestine from the Jordan Valley; it can be no longer identified, but it was still known in the days of Hosea (2.15). "Achor" means "trouble", and so 1 Chron. 2.7 changes Achan's name to Achar, the Troubler. It is the troubling of Jesus Christ on the cross that really creates a door of hope for humanity. There are grounds for thinking that it was Achan's sin that started the cleavage between Judah and the other tribes. The desolate mound of Jericho was the abiding memorial of Canaanite sin; the cairn in the Valley of Achor that of Achan's.

Joshua 8

This portion gives the story of the fourth lasting memorial erected by the Israelites in Canaan. The stone circle at Gilgal testified to God's faithfulness, the mound of Jericho to Canaan's sin, the cairn in the

Valley of Achor to Judah's sin, and the ruins of Ai to the sin of the people's self-confidence.

Now, even though they had the right to expect God's blessing, they used a very simple stratagem to gain a complete victory. The knowledge that God is on your side is no reason why you should not use the sense God has given you. God does most of His wonders through His gifts to men, once they are surrendered to Him.

The chapter introduces us to problems we cannot answer. The ruins of Ai that have been dug up were destroyed before 2000 B.C.—*i.e.*, in or before the time of Abraham. It may be that tradition has attached the name Ai to the wrong site, or that it had been so recently re-occupied that what was left of Joshua's destruction was washed away by heavy rains.

More important is the problem of Shechem. Nothing is said of the capture of the area between Ai and Shechem, because the population was very thin, without walled cities. It was only shortly before the Conquest that the means had been discovered for making the cisterns hewn in the limestone rock watertight. Until these had become general, in parts where there were no perennial springs there could be no great density of population. In contrast Shechem was an ancient town and we are told nothing of its capture. Yet the complete people (33,35) held a service just outside its gates (*cf.* also 24.1). It is probable that when the city came into Jacob's hands (Gen. 34), he gave it to a related group of Habiru (Hebrews), who may already have had some faith in Jehovah. When Israel entered Canaan, they will have linked up with them. This would explain the language of Judg. 9, where the citizens of Shechem are Israelites, but feel themselves superior to Israel. The law written on the plaster of the altar (*cf.* Deut. 27.2) was probably the law of Deut. 12—26. It was certainly not the whole Law.

Questions for Further Study and Discussion on Joshua chapters 1—8.

1. How does the teaching of Joshua chapter 1 compare with the Christian ideal of leadership given in Mark 10.42—45?
2. What can we learn about the principles of guidance from the account of the crossing of Jordan?
3. What is the significance of the fact that God did not punish the inhabitants of Canaan in the way that He did those of Sodom and Gomorrah?
4. How far does ch. 7 throw light on the story of Ananias and Sapphira (Acts 5.1—11)?
5. How do we relate the story of the events at Ai to the general question of discipline in the Christian Church?

9

Rahab (ch. **2**) both feared Jehovah and trusted Him, so she was able to save her life and that of her family as free persons. The leaders of Gibeon's four-city confederation feared Jehovah, but did not trust Him, so they saved their lives but became slaves (27).

Israel was on its guard. Its leaders were not going to come to terms with any local people (7), but they knew that they were allowed to with those at a distance, outside the promised land (Deut. **20**.10—15). The deceit used was fairly transparent, but a judicious touch of flattery guaranteed that the obvious questions would not be put. There is always something heartwarming for most of us when we hear that God's dealings with us are being spoken of by people at a distance. If we remember how unimportant the most important of us are, we are likely to be suspicious of those who sing our praises without having known us.

The most important lesson of this chapter is its warning that there are actions we can commit as Christians which we cannot retract. The Gibeonite confederation lay strategically at a most important point, especially while Jerusalem lay in Jebusite hands. It is not surprising that Saul in his "zeal for Israel" tried to eliminate this foreign population (2 Sam. **21**.2). He succeeded in forcing the population of Beeroth to emigrate (2 Sam. **4**.2,3). The price he had to pay was first the assassination of his son Ishbosheth (2 Sam. **4**.7), and then the judicial execution of seven sons and grandsons (2 Sam. **21**.8,9). The severity of the punishment, quite apart from the seven years of drought on Israel, which he officially represented before God, indicates the enormity of his sin. The final picture we have of Gibeon is that it had become the great high place of Israel (1 Ki. **3**.4, 2 Chron. **1**.3,5).

The most obvious example of a responsibility we take on ourselves without having the right to terminate it is marriage. There are many aching and impoverished Christian hearts because natural desire was accepted as an indication of God's will. But we must look further. Our promises do not need the strengthening of an oath to be binding (Matt. **5**.37). No Christian has the right to break a promise because it suits him (Psa. **15**.4). If we feel that we have made a major mistake, we must pray for grace to glorify God in the mistake.

Joshua 10

Gibeon's action gave Israel a firm grip on the centre of the hills; this thoroughly alarmed the main towns in the area. Immediately Israel had to learn that a partner not chosen by God was an unreliable ally. But just because Israel remained true to his promise, where it seemed a gain not to, God gave him special help.

The "great stones from heaven" (11) are hailstones. We then have a quotation from a book of poetry—*The Book of Jashar* (*cf.* 2 Sam. 1.18) is one of Israel's lost books; it would seem to have been a collection of old national poems. Being poetry, it is hard to interpret, and various explanations are offered of the exact miracle described in vs. 12,13, but that a miracle happened is clear. A full discussion by E. W. Maunder, a former Astronomer Royal, may be found in *The Astronomy of the Bible* or *The International Standard Bible Encyclopedia*. He points out that from Gibeon *via* Beth-horon to Azekah and Makkedah (10) is twenty-seven miles, far more than could have been covered by fighting men in the time; in addition they had time to capture the city (28). The most reasonable explanation of v. 15 is that it ends the account of the victory with that of the victorious return, though the mopping-up operation must have happened before it (16—28).

These verses create difficulties just because of the completeness of the mopping-up. It is very hard to reconcile the account of complete annihilation with 14.6—15, 15.13—19, Judg. 1.8—15. The difficulty lies not in an apparent reconquest, but in the need of one after such a complete massacre of the population; even had some survived, they could not have increased enough in the interval. The most likely explanation is that we have here the account of a "combined operation". As Judah marched south (see notes on Judg. 1), Joshua swept round the coastal plain, and the country was caught in a pincers' operation. Because Joshua was the over-all general who had done the planning, the whole campaign is described as his work. The cave at Makkedah can be regarded as the fifth of Israel's monuments, this time of his greatest victory.

Joshua 11

When the Israelite occupation moved north of Shechem, they were faced by a line of fortresses cutting them off from the great plain of Esdraelon, Jezreel, or Megiddo (17.11—13; Judg. 1.27), but light-armed troops, like those of the Israelites, could slip between them very easily, especially at night. It was probably their infiltration into the plain that alarmed Jabin, king of Hazor (1). On older maps the name "Waters of Merom" (5) is generally put against the small lake north

11

of the Sea of Galilee. Modern maps call this Lake Huleh and link the waters of Merom with Merom in the heart of Galilee. Israel's sudden attack was the more effective because the chariots could not be used in the hill country. They had been brought for a battle in the plain.

If we put vs. 12,13 together, we find that Israel destroyed the weaker towns that could be rushed, but left the stronger ones, except Hazor, uncaptured. This was particularly serious and inexcusable in the case of the cities mentioned in 12.21—23, whose kings had been killed. The probable reason is that the people were getting tired of fighting (cf. 18). Since only the highlights of the Conquest are given us, we are apt to think it was much shorter than it was in fact. Christians are always in most danger when they feel tired and think it does not matter whether or not they complete their task. It was just these cities that created one of the most serious dangers in the period of the Judges (Judg. 4,5).

"The Negeb" (16; 10.40—today, Negev) means all the land south of Hebron and Lachish down to the limits of cultivation. Owing to the uncertain rainfall agriculture is hazardous and much of the area is left to semi-nomads. The Anakim (21), or sons of Anak, were the remains of a particularly tall tribe among the earlier settlers in Canaan. They made the spies think of the pre-Flood giants (Num. 13.33; cf. Deut. 9.2). They were probably not very formidable, for they had already so dwindled as not to be mentioned among the peoples of Canaan (Gen. 15.19—21), unless, indeed, they are the same as the Rephaim. It is always the same; we tend to judge by looks.

Joshua 12

If at all possible, study this chapter with a good Bible map beside you. Better still, draw an outline map of Palestine, marking the places mentioned, making a difference between places captured and those where the town was left, even though the king was killed.

In vs. 1—6 we have a summary of Num. 21.21—35; 32.1—42. "The Arabah" (1,3,8) is here the Jordan Valley from the Sea of Galilee southwards; the term is sometimes confined to the more desert portions round the Dead Sea and south of it. "The Sea of Chinneroth" (3)—i.e., the Sea of Galilee; the name is probably derived from kinnor, a harp, there being a similarity in the shape.

"Mount Halak" (7), the Bald Mountain, site unknown; it is just possible that "Baal-gad" may be Baalbek. The lowland (8)—i.e., the Shephelah, or low hills between the central hills and the coastal plain. For the Israelite living in the hills they were low, the more so as he had given up hope of conquering the plains. The "slopes": a term is used which cannot be identified with certainty. It probably refers to the steep slope down to the Jordan Valley and the Dead Sea. "Goiim in Galilee" (23): R.S.V. is almost certainly correct in following the Greek with Galilee, rather than the Hebrew with Gilgal. "Goiim" means nations, but it is likely that Harosheth-ha-goiim (Judg. 4.2) is intended.

It would be unfair to suggest that the Church is unwilling to thank God for all His many mercies, but on the whole it is unwilling to indulge in detailed and specific thanks. If we were to train ourselves to recognize God's goodness act by act and detail by detail, many of us would come to think more highly both of God and of the Church. Much of our despondency comes from failing to see how much God has really achieved. On the other hand, such detailed thanksgiving would also make us more detailedly conscious of what had not been attained. Experience shows that the more we turn our attention to God's acts, the more we are aware of our falling short. This list is an excellent example, because it repeatedly reminds us of how much had been left undone, in spite of God's mighty acts.

Joshua 13.1—14.5

We may be surprised at the great detail in this section of *Joshua* (chs. 13—21), but these are the title-deeds of the children of Israel. Whatever the later fate of a tribe, its members could always say, "This is the land that God has given us." Where enemies had conquered it in whole or in part, the record stood as a reproach and a testimony to sin.

Read vs. 1—6 with Judg. 3.1—4. This is not a complete list of the unconquered, but of those God did not intend to be conquered by the first generation. It is always God's will that we should leave something for those that follow us to do. They lay not in the land but round it. Because the Israelites did not conquer what they should have, they never fully conquered these extra territories, but only made them tributary, and some (the Phoenician territory, 6) not at all.

We are told that half-Manasseh did not conquer Geshur and Maacath (13). The former is the region to the east of the Sea of Galilee, the latter the eastern slopes of the upper Jordan Valley leading up to Mt. Hermon. Absalom's mother was a daughter of the king of Geshur (2 Sam. 3.3; 13.37). Psalm 42 was written by one who lived near or in Maacath (6); it gives a picture of the rude and godless people that grew up in the mixed frontier area.

The treatment of the Levites (14) had a deeply practical motive.

Whenever the holding of a religious office is made to depend mainly on birth and not on special religious qualifications it will gradually accumulate power in the hands of the family concerned, so that it will gradually become a threat to the good of society. God made hereditary the position of the Aaronic priest and of the Levite, but put a limit on their ability to become rich.

The difference between the two-and-a-half tribes east of Jordan and those west of the river is that those east asked for what they wanted (Num. 32.1—5)—this is not directly stated of half-Manasseh but we can assume they made their wishes clear enough. The rest accepted what God gave them. Already in ch. 22 we find the former beginning to wonder whether they had not made a mistake. Certainly their lands were always most open to attack.

Joshua 14.6—15.12

There are no grounds, once we realize that Hebrew historical writing is not tied by strict chronological order, for placing 14.6 after 13.1—14.5, or even after ch. 12. It seems impossible not to link it with Judg. 1.1b—20. This can be placed best, though without certainty, after the sin of Achan and the capture of Ai; this in turn would permit "the pincers' movement" suggested in the notes on ch. 10. As is clear from 18.1, Judah's lot was allocated before the general partition, as were also those of Ephraim and half-Manasseh (16.1). We no longer know why, but priority in God's giving does not imply favouritism. If Judah was to go up first against the Canaanites (Judg. 1.1), it was only fair that he should have his portion first.

Caleb made a discovery that many others have made. The exercise of his faith acted as a kind of general tonic. It is not that faith always cures physical weaknesses, but it is a marvellous help towards making the maximum use of what God has given us. Many complain of weakness and lack of gifts because they have never learnt by faith to use what they have. Caleb is specially mentioned in connection with Judah, because he was not an Israelite but a Kenizzite (14), from one of the Midianite clans. It was fitting that the foreigner should have been received into Judah, for "to him shall be the obedience of the peoples" (Gen. 49.10).

With what loving care the boundary of Judah is traced! Were it not that some of the place-names cannot be identified with absolute certainty, we could draw the frontier on the ground today. It is exact even in the most unlikely places. The South boundary runs through desert, where it might be claimed that frontier delimitation was of no importance, but it is accurately given for all that. Note that the Valley of Achor is within Judah's bounds (7). Very many Christians have no interest in discovering what God has given them and therefore never enjoy it. In addition they spend much of their time in coveting or trying to cultivate the possessions of others. This is one of the most potent sources of Christian dissatisfaction.

Many a collision between Christians comes because they try to use the same track.

Joshua 15.13—63

The first part of our reading continues the story of Caleb (see also Judg. 1.10—15). From the latter we see that this was no isolated campaign by Caleb. He belonged now to Judah and together with Judah he fought. Othniel was his nephew; such marriages were at the time both common and favoured (*cf.* Gen. 20.12, 24.47, 29.15—19). Those Greek MSS that read "he urged her" (18) are probably correct. *Field* in the O.T. normally means open country, in many cases untilled because it was unsuitable. Presumably the area round the springs (19) is meant. For Negeb see note on 11.16.

Most of the latter part (20—62) is an appendix put in by a later editor giving the organization of Judah under the monarchy after the time of Solomon. Solomon, for various practical reasons, was not able to use the old tribal boundaries. He divided the land into twelve portions, normally near the old divisions (1 Kings 4.7—19; vs. 13 and 19 refer to the same region, Geber having been replaced by his son). When the kingdom was split under Rehoboam, Judah was divided into twelve administrative districts to emphasize its claims to remain the true Israel, even if the Northern Kingdom bore the name. The paragraph division in R.S.V. is intended to bring this out, but it is in one point misleading. A very little study should convince you that vs. 45—47 belong together. For all that, there are twelve sections, for after v. 59 in Hebrew a group of towns has fallen out; it has been preserved in the Greek—*viz.* "Tekoa, and Ephrath (the same is Bethlehem), and Peor, and Etam, and Kolon, and Tatam, and Sores, and Kerem, and Gallim, and Bether, and Manahath; eleven cities and their villages." These eleven form the tenth section. Only in the fifth section (45—47) is no number of places given, and that because the section is mainly imaginary. It consists of the Philistine land which Judah failed to hold at the first (*cf.* Judg. 1.18,19). David was able to make it tributary, but already under Solomon the Philistines had freed themselves, and so this section remained a dream and a grief.

15

V. 63 is a second appendix. Jerusalem was virtually reckoned to Judah (see note on ch. 18 at end). In Judg. 1 we are told how Judah did not deal adequately with Jerusalem, because it was not in its portion; now it was a thorn in its flesh. This was one of the causes helping towards the split under Rehoboam.

Questions for Further Study and Discussion on Joshua chapters 9—15.

1. How does the story of Israel and the Gibeonites (ch. 9) apply to the people of God today?
2. "Israel's greatest victory (ch. 10) was won defending those who had put their trust in them." What does this imply for us?
3. In what sense may "giants" left over from the past (ch. 11) trouble us in the Christian life?
4. Trace the theme of the hardening of men's hearts, from chapter 11, v. 20, through Exod. 4.21, Isa. 6.10, Matt. 13.13—15, and Rom. 9.17*f*.
5. What is the tribute frequently paid to Caleb's character (ch. 14)? How far is the refusal to rest on one's past achievements an ingredient of true faith?

Joshua 16,17

If we can see some reason why Judah received his portion in advance, none is apparent for "the descendants of Joseph" (16.1). It is not unreasonable to suppose that the pride of Ephraim, which becomes so prominent in *Judges* and which finds an earlier expression in 17.14, lay behind it.

Reuben was Jacob's first-born, and therefore the birthright of a double portion in the inheritance was his. By his sin he forfeited his right (1 Chron. 5.1,2), which automatically went to Joseph as firstborn of Jacob's other wife. This meant in turn that in the distribution of the land the descendants of Joseph were entitled to two portions. This was not done by giving both Ephraim and Manasseh a portion, for it is here clearly said that the allotment was to the descendants of Joseph, who divided it among them. The birthright was satisfied by giving Manasseh, the first-born of Joseph, an extra portion (17.1,5,6,17)—*viz.*, east of Jordan. For 17.3 see Num. 27.1—7.

The arrogance of the Joseph tribes is seen in 17.16. They were not prepared to bring the hill country under cultivation (see note on ch. 8 for the reason why it was thinly populated—without adequate water supply it had not been worth clearing the forest trees and scrub) and were equally unprepared to conquer the plain. In addition they had been given what was in many ways the best part of the country. 17.11—13 suggests a particular act of meanness. It seems that Issachar and Asher had voluntarily ceded part of their territory, because they felt they could not tackle the strong fortresses. Manasseh accepted the territory, but did little to dislodge the Canaanites. Note the subtle difference between 16.10 and 17.12; Manasseh *could* not, but Ephraim *would* not. In fact Gezer did not become Israelite until the time of Solomon, and then it was the dowry Pharaoh gave his daughter (1 Kings 9.16).

"The chariots of iron" (16,18) were wooden chariots strengthened with iron plates—they could be burnt (11.6,9). It was not the actual chariots that dismayed the Israelites but the differing concept of war that lay behind their use. They were based on stable lines of infantry, while the Israelites fought as irregulars, who could easily be cut to pieces by the quickly moving chariots.

Joshua 18

We are inevitably heirs of the past, and so was Israel. Some of their most important towns were already old when Abraham saw them. But their religion, in spite of resemblances in the sacrificial ritual, had nothing to do with Canaan's past. Archaeology has shown that Shiloh was first built by Israel. They wanted their chief sanctuary untainted by memories of Canaanite religion. At first, it seems clear, "the tent of meeting" was moved around a certain amount. Was it at Shechem at 24.1? It was at Bethel in Judg. 20.27,28. Finally in 1 Samuel 1 we find a temple at Shiloh. Excavations have shown it to have been the same size as the Tent. Probably this was still standing, but a building would have been erected around it to protect it from the elements.

The slackness blamed by Joshua (3) may well have been due to an unwillingness to settle down. It was fine to have a "promised land", but the reality showed the need for learning new skills and engaging in hard work. That is for many the disappointing side of God's gifts; they are always given that we may serve the better. Even His rest is linked with a yoke (Matt. 11.28—30).

Joshua, in his God-given wisdom, did not allow himself to be involved in the distribution of the land beyond presiding at the casting of the lots (10). The tribal portions were not arbitrary, but represented real natural divisions of the country, even though modern methods of transport have often hidden that fact.

17

Even though the division of the seven portions was by lot, God clearly overruled it, so that tribes which had reasons for feeling close to one another were normally together. Benjamin, the other Rachel tribe, accordingly found itself next to the Joseph portion. These boundaries are not to be regarded as unchangeable frontiers. We have in this list an apparent contradiction. "Kiriath-jearim", under the name of Kiriath-baal, is in v. 14 allocated to Judah (*cf.* 15.60), but in v. 28 it is claimed as Benjaminite. The border may have fluctuated a mile or two. In this case, however, it may be linked with the fact that the other three towns of the Gibeonite four-city confederation were on Benjaminite territory (25,26). The memories of the original inhabitants may, for the time being, have been more potent than the official demarcation. Benjamin also owned an uncaptured Jerusalem.

Joshua 19

We gain the impression that here we have to do with one of the worst bits of sharp practice in the Bible. "The portion of the tribe of Judah was too large for them" (9): yet it had been allocated to them by God! In fact, though Judah had the largest area west of Jordan, so much of it was desert or poor pasture land that effectively it was probably no larger than any other. The Simeonite towns will be found in the first (15.28,29,30,31,32) and fourth (15.42) divisions of Judah; the position was reasonably fertile, but lay along Judah's weakest frontier. Judah had failed to hold the coastal plain; now he was willing that Simeon should be a shield against eventualities. In v. 2 read with Greek, Beer-sheba, Shema (*cf.* 15.26) . . . ; there is a name too many. In v. 7 add Tochen (*cf.* 1 Chron. 4.32). As a result Simeon found it very hard to keep a separate existence, and Judah found itself without its shield (*cf.* Judg. 15.11, 1 Sam. 27.6).

In the description of Zebulon's lot it is clear that the names of seven towns have dropped out at the beginning of v. 15; Jokneam, Kartah, and Dimnah can be supplied from 21.35. The Bethlehem mentioned is, of course, not the better-known one in Judah.

The reason why the boundaries of Issachar and Asher are only partially given is explained by 17.11; the handing over of certain towns to Manasseh made the drawing of an exact boundary impossible. The extension of Asher's boundaries to Sidon (28) and Tyre (29) is again an ideal; it is doubtful whether they ever held the territory. At the time Sidon was more important than Tyre. It seems obvious that "Judah" (34) is a scribal error. This and others are due to the inherent difficulty in copying out little-known names.

Several of Dan's cities (41) will be found in the second division of Judah (15.33), while Ekron is claimed by them both. With the withdrawal of the Danites these cities, when conquered by Judah, are included in its territory. For v. 47, *cf.* Judg. 18. It is not clear whether all the tribe of Dan moved, but probably not. The failure of Dan to maintain its position was mainly due to Judah's failure to hold the coastal plain. Because Dan never really occupied its area, its boundary is not given.

Joshua 20

This chapter must be read in the light of Num. 35.9—28. In particular "until he has stood before the congregation for judgment" (6, also 9) is explained by Num. 35.24,25.

Man can never restore life, once he has taken it, and so the Bible regards even innocent manslaughter as a major fault, and so does not forbid the age-old custom of the avenger of blood. The Law protects the innocent man but inflicts a very heavy penalty. Not only had he to leave home, but he was confined to the bounds of the city of refuge (Num. 35.26,27), probably a distance of two thousand cubits—*i.e.*, a thousand yards—from the walls (Num. 35.4,5). For an agriculturist, with no skill as an artisan, this must have been most irksome. The making of the high priest's death the limit of time during which he was at the avenger's mercy, if he left the city, was partly due to the fact that the high priest was the only regular official personage at the time. At the same time there is a veiled type pointing to Jesus Christ, the great high priest. The lying-in-wait at the city boundaries was equally irksome for the avenger, so we may be sure that many cases were settled by a money payment.

Unfortunately this was one of the laws which were little observed in the wild period of the Judges. There is no suggestion in 2 Sam. 3.26—39 that Abner should have been safe in Hebron. Equally David did not suggest to the widow from Tekoa (2 Sam. 14.4—11) that a city of refuge was the solution of her problem. It was not until royal power and justice grew strong that true justice could be enforced.

All six cities, as commanded by Moses (Num. 35.6), were Levitical cities. This was doubtless to ensure a fairer first hearing, when the man reached the city (4). To increase the effectiveness of the cities, apparently such were chosen as already had a certain sanctity. The cities east of Jordan are too little known to us for an opinion to be given, but "Kedesh" (7) itself means "holy", Shechem was marked out by the great post-Conquest covenant renewal (ch. 24), and

Hebron was bound up with memories of Abraham and his walk with God.

God's very stress on the sanctity of human life should increase our sense of awe at the sacrifice of Jesus Christ.

Joshua 21

By the giving of cities to the Levites we must understand, not that they were inhabited exclusively by Levites—they quite obviously were not—but that they were afforded adequate room within the walls to build their houses (*cf.* Lev. 25.32—34). Then the land up to a thousand yards in every direction belonged to them (Num. 35.5,6), though, apparently, they were to use it for grazing purposes only, not for agriculture. This was to remind them that their stake in the land was a different one (18.7).

God's overruling of the lot is seen particularly in the descendants of Aaron (13—18). Not only were they well placed for the temple that would be in Jerusalem, but with the division of the kingdom they found themselves automatically in Judah. For Anathoth (18) *cf.* 1 Kings 2.26, Jer. 1.1.

This dispersal of the Levites ensured that in every tribe there would be some who were specially acquainted with the Law and would be able to teach it. Even more important was that they were inextricably bound up with the fortunes of the people. In our highly organized modern society it is all too easy for the believer to live to himself, washing his hands of his unbelieving neighbours. Not so in Israel. A number of the towns will be recognized as having remained un-conquered, so some of the Levites remained homeless for a long time. In the case of Gezer (21) they had to wait until the time of Solomon, and even then they found only smoking ruins (1 Kings 9.16). Gibeon, with its Canaanite population, became a priestly town (*cf.* 1 Kings 3.4, 2 Chron. 1.3,5), so they were constantly reminded of the fault of their ancestors. When invaders, pestilence, drought came over part of the land because of the people's sin, there were always some Levites involved.

If you will mark the Levitical cities in the measure your map allows, you will see that the tribal giving was generous. They allotted some of the choicest sites in the land to them—*e.g.*, Hebron, Libnah, Debir, Gibeon, Shechem, Taanach, Kadesh, Jokneam, Ramoth-Gilead, Mahanaim, Heshbon.

At long last the time for return home had come, and the long labour of the two-and-a-half tribes had finished. They had paid a heavy price for their choice of territory, even if they went back rich (8). But it was not until they reached the Jordan that they fully realized what they had done. While, presumably, there were no particular difficulties in crossing, yet they saw what a barrier it really was, and how easily those on the other side could be thought of as living in another land. That they were not mistaken is shown by the language of the rest of the people, when they heard of the building of the altar (12); "on the side that belongs to the people of Israel" is a phrase that virtually disowned the people on the other side.

The making of the altar was not in itself forbidden at that time. But there had been no appearance of God, no theophany, to justify it (Deut. 12.5,11,14,18—language which envisages the possibility of God's choosing more than one place, as in fact He did). Then it was an ostentatiously large altar (10) and a copy of the one in Shiloh (28). In the rash judgment of the other tribes it was the setting up of "non-conformist" worship. They did not stop to think that the altar was on the wrong side of the Jordan for that. If we would only stop to think at times, we would realize that actions we disapprove of may in fact have other explanations than the apparently obvious ones.

It is striking that it was an altar they erected as the symbol of their unity with their brothers. They knew that the only real link between them was spiritual. It has today come to be realized more fully than earlier that, until the rise of the monarchy, the tribes were in fact independent units. It was their loyalty to one God and to one central sanctuary that bound them together in a union, the efficiency of which depended on the reality of their faith at any given time. In fact the eastern tribes seem to have backslidden less than some in the west. No special acts of idolatry are recorded of them, and in the dark hours under Ahab it was from Gilead that Elijah came (1 Kings 17.1).

Joshua 23

There are many who think that this chapter and the next describe the same event; this is quite likely, because the Bible is not averse to such descriptions from differing standpoints. Such an interpretation will not affect our understanding of the chapter.

"All Israel" (2) is, unless the opposite is clearly stated (e.g., 8.35), always to be understood in such contexts of the whole people as represented by their leaders.

The first main point is a positive one (6,8), that they must remain true to God's revelation, as they had received it. It is not enough to keep from evil; one must positively do good in the way it has been revealed.

The second is the danger of compromise. The day was to come when Jesus Christ was to demonstrate by the power of the Holy Spirit that He could move among the worst of men and yet keep Himself "unstained from the world" (Jas. 1.27). Until then it was God's will for His people that they should be separate from the heathen—stories like those of Daniel show that God's power was sufficient to keep His loyal ones, when the lack of separation was not of their choosing. The history of Israel in the O.T. is less one of apostasy and more one of compromise with heathen neighbours; this led in turn to a worship which God refused to accept as being in any sense worship of Him at all.

The third is the need of loving God (11). As in the N.T. the love should be based on what God has done (9,10). No mere separation and mechanical keeping of God's will can ever be adequate. It is the attraction of God that drives out the attraction of the surroundings.

The fourth is a warning against intermarriage (12,13). The story of Ruth is evidence enough that there was no mere nationalistic or racial prejudice behind the warning. But Ruth had come to love God, thanks to the example Naomi had set her, before she ever met Boaz. In marriage man and wife become "one flesh" in a new union, and to this both contribute, probably fairly equally. It is useless one or the other thinking that love will lead the other to Christ. The believer can give all in the marriage, but the unbeliever will also contribute his or her all. The believer cannot lift the partner to salvation, but the unbeliever will go far in making unbelief the dominant factor.

Joshua 24

In this chapter the need of determined choice is stressed. Joshua knew that it was better to choose wrong than not to choose at all. The man who is never sure, who does not know his ideals, his loyalties, his beliefs, is like a half-dead fish floating all the time downstream. Joshua held out three choices to Israel.

First there were the gods their ancestors had worshipped before Abram ever heard and followed the voice of God (2,15). In v. 14 it is made clear, what in any case was obvious, that Joshua was not suggesting a revival of the past. Whatever may have been true of the leading Patriarchs, Gen. **35**.2—4 was for most participants a merely outward ceremony.

The next possibility was the adoption of the gods of the conquered people (15). It is true that they had shown themselves powerless in the presence of Jehovah, but at least they claimed to be thoroughly modern and "scientific". They promised a true control over agriculture, fertility, and sex generally. Even though they had been defeated and largely annihilated, the peoples of Canaan felt themselves intellectually and culturally miles ahead of the Israelites.

The third and real possibility was Jehovah. In vs. 3—13 Joshua stressed the goodness and power of God. His very greatness made single-minded loyalty essential (14). We may find it hard to believe that old loyalties could persist over such a momentous four centuries, but that is the way with men. It is remarkable how much of mediaeval Catholicism, and even old paganism, lies hidden in much modern Protestantism. The answer of the people was an obvious one. They protested that they had no intention of serving anyone but Jehovah (16—18). The evangelist can overlook that under certain circumstances and in certain surroundings his message can be accepted as obvious. So Joshua told them brutally that they could not serve Jehovah (19). Conversion is the work of the Holy Spirit. The type of life God demands (not merely expects) from the regenerate is a supernatural one, which only the Holy Spirit can create.

For vs. 29, 30 cf. **19**.49,50, Judg. **2**.8,9.

Questions for Further Study and Discussion on Joshua chapters 16—24.

1. What weaknesses in Israel are shown by **16**.10 and **17**.12,13?
2. What is the contemporary spiritual counterpart to Israel's failure (**15**.63, **16**.10, **17**.12f.)?
3. Study carefully Joshua's answer to the complaint of the Joseph-tribes (**17**.14—18) and analyse the qualities which it revealed.
4. What is the relationship of the story in ch. **19** to the principle defined in Gal. **6**.5?
5. We learn a great deal about the geography of Palestine from chs. **13**—**21**; we can admire the wisdom of God in the way He arranged matters. What lessons can we reasonably deduce—by analogy, not allegory—for the Church today?
6. Relate your reading in Joshua ch. **22** to the matter of Christian unity today.
7. What in ch. **24** is the sin above all others that Joshua warned against? Why does Scripture condemn it so severely?

Judges

INTRODUCTION

Judges is anonymous, just as is *Joshua*. Very much of it is very old and even contemporaneous with the events described, but the book as such does not seem to have received its final form till the reign of Ahaz or Hezekiah; *cf.* **18**.30 with 2 Kings **15**.29.

The book is not a history of the period, but **3**.7—**16**.31 give us an account of God's power in deliverance through the "Judges". It should be remembered that there is no real claim made to chronological order. Several of the Judges could have been contemporaries. This heart of the book is preceded by a section (**1**.1—**3**.6) explaining how the troubles came to happen and is followed by two appendices (chs. **17,18** and **19**—**21**) showing some of the disorders that could exist at the time.

Judges 1.1—2.5

This portion is largely Israel's roll of dishonour, a record of what it left undone. For its understanding we must grasp that "After the death of Joshua" (**1**.1) is the name of the book as a whole. The death of Joshua is not given till **2**.8,9, and it is clear that the incidents in ch. **1** are all, or almost all, from his lifetime.

For vs. 8—20 see notes on Josh. **14**.6 and **15**.13, and for the campaign in general those on **10**.29—38. The easiest explanation of vs. 1,2 is that the sin of Achan caused such bitter feelings against his tribe that God saw fit to separate Judah for the time being from his comrades. We know nothing of Bezek nor of Adoni-bezek, so we can throw no extra light on vs. 4—7. The fact that he was brought to Jerusalem is no hint that he was its king (*cf.* Josh. **10**.1). "The city of palms" (16): see note on Josh. **6**. There is no need to see any link between v. 17 and Num. **21**.1—3. "Hormah" means "Put in the ban" or "Given over to destruction". Actually there was a considerable distance between the two sites. For vs. 18,19 see note on Josh. **15**.45—47.

Judah and Simeon had burnt Jerusalem (8), but evidently because it was not in their territory they could not be bothered to do the job

24

properly. By the time Benjamin tried it was too late. Though not strong enough to form a physical frontier, Jerusalem created a psychological one which helped increasingly to separate Judah from the North.

Mark the uncaptured cities, so far as you are able, on a map. It may surprise you to see what a strategic position they occupy. Just as Jerusalem helped to isolate the South, so did the towns along Esdraelon Galilee.

"The angel of the Lord" (2.1) should probably here be rendered "The messenger of the Lord"—*i.e.*, a prophet. Hebrew MSS indicate that there is a gap in v. 1 after "he said". Although we are so near the Conquest, we have already reached one of the turning-points in Israel's history. The people might weep and sacrifice, but God never permitted them, from then on, even when they captured *some* of the unconquered cities, to clear out their inhabitants. In other words, Israel never reached the limits of even a more restricted land, and they never had it entirely to themselves.

Judges 2.6—3.6

"Baal" means in itself "owner" and could be used for any god who was considered to be in some special way owner of a place or district. By the Israelite period it had come to mean especially the sky-god who was the bringer of the rains. Owing to the vital importance of rain for Palestine, he had become the most important of the Canaanite gods. Ashtoreth (plural "*Ashtaroth*", 13) was the great goddess of the earth and fertility. The prophetic writers of the Bible were not interested in introducing their readers to the rather bloody and distinctly pornographic details of Canaanite mythology. They simply lumped all the male gods together as Baals, the female ones normally as Ashtaroth; but see 3.7.

That is not all. The gods of the Canaanites were all Nature gods—*i.e.*, they were the spirits that made Nature work and were ultimately subject to the laws of Nature. Jehovah was the Creator of Nature, outside it and its Controller. Every effort to regard Him as greater than, but in some way like, the Canaanite gods so lowered Him that the writers call that Baal-worship also. There is little evidence for a complete abandonment of Jehovah-worship or of the independent worship of the Canaanite gods. It was, however, obvious that such a god would use other gods to help him out, and that he would have a

25

wife. So other deities were honoured beside Jehovah. This is the background suggested in 2.11—13; but *cf.* 10.6.

A judge (*shophet*) is not one who enforces the law, but one who is a deliverer. It is in this sense that Israel's deliverers are called judges. Since they were deliverers because the Spirit of God rested on them, they will afterwards have been called in to act as judges in a more literal sense. Since law cases at this time were all civil ones—*i.e.*, the person wronged brought an action against the one who had wronged him, and perjury was looked on with much more indulgence than with us—it often needed spiritual wisdom to discover the truth. 1 Kings 3.16—28 gives us an example of Israelite judicial wisdom at its highest.

Question: How can the "down-grading" of God be practised by Christians today?

Judges 3.7–31

The first judge is Othniel; after his time Judah ceases to play any significant part in the book, except in the second appendix. "Mesopotamia" (8): more likely northern Syria than the area east of the Euphrates. The oppressor's name means "Cushan Double-Wickedness". This is obviously a playful pun on his real name. The first judgment was a warning and came from one at a distance, whose existence was independent of the completeness or incompleteness of the Conquest.

"Asheroth" (7): plural of Asherah. Asherah was a Canaanite goddess, and so the plural can be used like Ashtaroth (2.13) for the female deities in general. It is occasionally used for an image of her (*e.g.*, 1 Kings 15.13, 2 Kings 23.7). Normally it means the sacred wooden pole erected in every Canaanite and Canaanite-type sanctuary, representing the female element in deity, even as the stone, or pillar (*mazzebah*), beside it represented the male element. A.V. (K.J.V.) "grove" is most misleading.

The fact that the next oppressor did not penetrate further into Israel than Jericho—for "the city of palm trees" (13) see note on Josh. 6—suggests that his burden affected almost entirely the Benjaminites, which is perhaps the reason why his tyranny was allowed to last for 18 years (14). Ehud's plan called for very careful timing. He had to obtain a private audience with Eglon on the pretext of a divine message. Gilgal (19) was not far from Jericho, and Eglon's guards may have seen him turn back there—at "the sculptured stones": perhaps an account of the crossing of the Jordan had been engraved on them (Josh. 4.20). Then he had to gain enough time not merely to save his own life, but also to seize the fords of Jordan before the Moabites could make up their mind what to do. The Moabites did not realize he was left-handed (cf. 20.16) and so did not suspect the sword at his right side. Note that the Ephraimites were ready to follow, but not to lead; we shall meet this trait again later.

There is no suggestion that Shamgar was an Israelite (cf. 5.6), nor is he introduced in the ordinary way. He was probably a Canaanite, for whom the Philistine penetration into the land was as unwelcome as for the Israelites. God is under no obligation to use one of His own people for the liberation of His people.

Judges 4

Now Israel's chickens have really come home to roost. The Canaanite cities of Galilee and the plain of Esdraelon had recovered from the mauling they had received in Joshua's day, and they threatened the whole of northern Israel. It looked as though the whole work of the Conquest might be nullified. The events are told us in two versions. The triumphal psalm (ch. 5), composed immediately after the victory, is put second, because the prose account (ch. 4), written a little later, gives us a more balanced, though also incomplete, picture of what happened. The two have to be put together.

In ch. 5 we see the campaign as a challenge to all Israel, to which some tribes respond. From ch. 4 it is clear that the real initiative lay with Zebulon and Naphtali (10, 5.18); Issachar, so far as his position in the plain allowed, probably also joined the main force (5.15). Barak, marching from Kedesh, led his forces almost past Jabin's capital (see map) and took up his position on Mt. Tabor (6), where Sisera could not ignore his presence. In fact Barak and his men were the bait in God's trap. Sisera hurriedly gathered his forces and marched to overwhelm him. Before he could attack, Barak's men rushed down on him (5.15) with the storm behind them. Half blinded by the rain the Canaanite ranks broke, and the chariots were bogged down in ground which was soft at the best of times (5.20,21). It will have been then that the other tribes attacked from the rear and the rout was complete.

While the broken army swept down the plain to Sisera's town at the gap where the Kishon flows towards the sea (16), Sisera turned desperately northwards (cf. 11), hoping probably that he could reach Hazor. Barak must soon have discovered that Sisera had escaped and turned north after him, only to find him dead (22).

It is often claimed that Jael was only protecting her honour. The men were away, doubtless hovering like vultures to strip the dead, and the only place where Sisera would be hidden was the women's portion of the tent (the men's lay open). Had he been found there by her husband on his return, it would have meant her death. This is true, but it is clear also that Jael did not share her husband's friendship for the Canaanites (17); it was her deliberate way of helping God's people, though it involved her in major risk.

Judges 5

The text of this ancient psalm has in places been poorly preserved. This helps to explain some of the striking differences between R.S.V. and A.V. (K.J.V.). It may well be that the N.E.B. Old Testament, when it appears, will contain other changes almost as striking.

In vs. 4,5 we do not have a picture of God coming to Israel's aid from Sinai, but a contrast between God's power as shown at the time of the Exodus and the grim reality of the recent past (6—8).

Judah and Simeon are not mentioned, because for them to have come would have been to imperil the secrecy essential to the whole operation. They would have had to march past Jerusalem, which could have sent an urgent message to Sisera. Machir (14) stands for Manasseh (Josh. 17.1), rather peculiarly, for he had settled in Bashan, and certainly the half-tribe west of Jordan is included. Gilead (17) stands for Gad. No tribe under the religious league then prevailing could be forced to come. But for a city within a tribe that had marched to withhold its help was another matter. That is why such a bitter curse is spoken against Meroz, a city of Manasseh (23). It implies that it had been put in the ban and would be destroyed. We can understand Asher and Dan; both were finding it hard to maintain their position at all. But Reuben and Gad illustrated the danger of being the other side of Jordan; they did not feel really involved.

The modern mind finds it hard to appreciate the barbaric satisfaction in Jael's act and the mockery of Sisera's mother. It was a hard and cruel time, and doubtless the hand of Sisera had been very heavy; v. 30 shows how they expected the Israelite villages to be looted after the victory. The real thing is that we are in the O.T. and in the period before the great prophets at that. God had still much to teach His people, and we need not be surprised that Deborah, though a prophetess, should have felt such satisfaction. Do not forget, either, that these people would not have existed if God's commands had been properly carried out at the Conquest.

Judges 6.1–35

Periodically, for reasons that remain unclear, the nomad population of the desert increases until there is an explosion. So it was in the time of Gideon. The Midianites and their allies (3) were specially helped by the fact that, though the camel had been used earlier, its full domestication had just been carried through. With their camels they swept up the Valley of Jezreel and through the plain of Esdraelon and finally down the coastal plain, but they could not go far in the real hills. They should have been checked by the line of cities covering the great trade route, but though they had lost their power through Deborah, they had not been captured; they probably looked on grimly, rejoicing that their Israelite neighbours were suffering more than they. Though it is not recorded, it must have been a specially difficult time for the tribes east of Jordan.

In estimating Gideon, do not take v. 15 too seriously; it is typical Oriental self-depreciation. Remember also 8.18,19. It seems fairly clear that in his dealings with the angel (11—22) Gideon sensed that he was in touch with the supernatural, but was not sure until the miracle took place. (Angels, who must not be mixed up with the cherubim, always appear in the normal form of men!) As the story develops, it becomes clear that his father is one of the leading personages in Ophrah. His is the altar (25), probably to Jehovah, worshipped as though He were a Canaanite god, because the care of the sanctuary, clearly a communal one, had been entrusted to him (28).

Gideon knew perfectly well that one or other of the servants would betray him quickly enough. We need not doubt that Joash had been very proud of the altar entrusted to him, but the prospect of losing a third, and possibly last, son made him quick-witted. We ought to apply his argument to our own circumstances. We are all too ready to defend God, where we think His honour is concerned. We should be far more ready to assume that God will look after His own honour, if our lives are such as to honour Him. The expression in v. 34 is particularly striking. Literally translated it is, "But the Spirit of the Lord clothed Himself in Gideon"; this did not mean the end of Gideon's personality.

We have already seen that Gideon was no reckless hero. He was willing to do God's will provided he was sure that it *was* God's will. The two signs asked for show how heavy the dew can be at certain times of year—the miraculous element does not lie in its quantity. The first sign was unnatural, but possible, because the fleece would be more likely to attract dew; the second surpasses man's understanding.

Gideon's camp was on the flanks of Mt. Gilboa (7.1). The first test put to his troops was in accordance with Scripture (Deut. 20.8), but in such a period of spiritual declension we may be sure that it had not been heard for a long time. "And Gideon tested them" (3): this translation is pure guess work; the Hebrew makes no sense at all. There seems to be no doubt that there has been a transposition in the Hebrew of v. 6. Those who lapped were those who went on all fours; those who put their hands to their mouth were those who knelt. There is no clear suggestion that there was any criterion of merit in the selection. Gideon was simply to choose whatever group was the smaller.

"He sent all the rest of Israel every man to his tent" (8) must be interpreted in the light of the sequel. Once the attack was launched there was no time for reinforcements; vs. 23,24 must have been prepared for before the battle, and similarly those sent off must have been told to hold themselves in readiness.

It would be interesting to know why Purah is specially mentioned (10,11). There must be some tale of great loyalty behind it. Gideon had done his part; now God showed him that He had been doing His. He had created among the Midianites this apparently irrational fear (14), which made them ready to panic at the slightest provocation. The braying of the rams' horns in the darkness, the war cries, and the lights would have tried better nerves than theirs. Once the camels panicked, all hope of a stand was gone. With every shadow an enemy, the initial death roll must have been terrible (22). The Midianite army scattered widely north and south in the Jordan valley.

Judges 7.24—8.32

In this portion we have an excellent example of how much of Israel's early history was written. There is a conflict between 7.25 and 8.4. It seems that the writer had two contemporary accounts before him. That in 7.24—8.3 was taken from one told in Ephraim; while 7.19—23, 8.4 *seq.* were taken from the story told in Ophrah. The writer so joined them as to leave an obvious and indeed self-explanatory seam.

It is important to note how God used Gideon's natural impulses. Zebah and Zalmunna, the great tribal kings, slept with an elite camel corps around them. They were far too well-disciplined to panic, and they were able to extricate themselves from the rout without difficulty. Others would have thought the job well done with the death of Oreb and Zeeb (literally Raven and Wolf), but the duty of revenge drove Gideon on until the two kings were in his hands.

The reluctance of Succoth (5) and Penuel (8) to help Gideon was due to the measure in which Trans-Jordan had been exposed to the Midianite peril. These cities had probably been able to maintain themselves only by humiliating treaties with the Midianites. Gideon's cruel treatment of them was probably because their whole policy had made it easier for the Midianites to cross the Jordan and raid unchecked.

Gideon refused to become the first king of Israel (23), but he was it, all but the title. Abimelech could assume (9.2) that his sons would succeed him in his position. Gideon made an ephod (27—however we understand this unexplained term, it must have been pretty solid to judge by the amount of gold that went into its making), thereby showing that he was prepared to make religious innovations, a power contemporaries attributed to kings. Then he had many wives (30), which was one of the standard ways in which kings distinguished themselves; we seldom find a commoner with more than two wives. So here we see the religious organization of the people already beginning to break down because of a fundamental lack of loyalty to Jehovah. Once the position with the Philistines became acute, the cry for a king would become so strong that God would give way.

We see also the mounting pride of Ephraim, which would ride for a fall, when a rougher man than Gideon met it (see **12**.1—6).

Judges 8.33—9.21

We are told this story, partly to give us a picture of society as it was breaking down when the check of true religion had virtually vanished, partly because of the lasting shock it gave to Israelite consciousness (*cf.* 2 Sam. **11**.21). We are probably intended also to see in it God's judgment on Gideon's pride, even if he was not prepared to take the final plunge and *call himself* king.

"Baal-berith" (33) means "Baal of the Covenant" and is the same as the El-berith of **9**.46. Clearly it is the God of Joshua's covenant (Josh. **24**.25) Who is being so worshipped, but with all sorts of Canaanite

31

corruptions. For Shechem see note on Joshua 8. The detail that all Abimelech's brothers were killed "upon one stone" (5) can only mean that this semi-pagan virtually offered them up as a human sacrifice to guarantee his kingdom. This will hardly have extended very far from Shechem itself. Most Israelites did not want to have anything to do with Abimelech, but equally they were not concerned with avenging the wrong done to Gideon's family (8.35).

Presumably Jotham's striking parable was given while they were still at the coronation ceremony. The point about it, which is often missed, is the complete uselessness of a king of the trees. All he can do is to "sway over" them (9,11,13), or act as "shade" for them (15), which, of course, the trees do not need. God is the king of the trees, and equally of Israel. So any king they can appoint can only be ornamental, an unneeded figure-head. To liken Abimelech to "the bramble" (14,15) was really an insult to the bramble, in spite of its weakness and treachery.

A careful reading of Israel's history will show that it was very rare for someone from a second-class marriage, like Abimelech (18), to rise to a position of leadership. A prophet might well do so, for in the sight of God all men stand equal. We can test it by finding whether the man's father is mentioned. Jotham knew that treachery begat treachery, and that there is very little honour among thieves, so he rightly foresaw that judgment would come from their own midst.

Judges 9.22–57

The two things by which men judged a king were whether he guaranteed justice and security on the roads. By acting as highwaymen the Shechemites gave Abimelech an extremely bad name. We are not told anything of Gaal's antecedents, but since birds of a feather flock together, he was probably leader of a bandit gang. We cannot fully understand his drunken boasts (28). Evidently the Shechemites chose to forget how they came to be in the city and claimed that they were descendants of Hamor (Gen. 34.2). "Did not the son of Jerubbaal ... serve the men of Hamor?" may be a reference to the help Abimelech received from the Shechemites.

Obviously Gaal was drunk (28), but Zebul, who can have had only a handful of armed men, realized that if he was allowed to take root in Shechem, he would soon be its lord. The next day the hardly sober Gaal had to face Abimelech's army (34—40) and was so badly mauled that Zebul's few men were able to expel him and the remainder of his band. The Shechemites thought the matter was settled, but they little knew "the bramble". They were his relations, while he needed them (2), but now he wiped them out (42—45).

"The Tower of Shechem" (46) seems to have been the fortress guarding the sanctuary, which was outside the walls of the town. Probably the people who took refuge there thought that they were claiming some sort of sanctuary, but by this time Abimelech cared as little for God as he did for relationship (46—49). Shechem occupied too important a site to remain long in ruins (*cf.* 1 Kings **12.1**).

Thebez is some little distance north of Shechem. It may have accepted Abimelech as king and now decided it had had enough of him, or he may have started a mad career of conquest. At any rate his treatment of Shechem called out a desperate resistance in which the women joined. A millstone well thrown crushed his skull, but proud and self-centred to the last he thought only of how to save his reputation. As 2 Samuel **11.21** shows us, his desperate gesture was in vain. There was no one to take over the reins of power he had dropped, and the thought of kingship slipped for the moment once more into the background.

What are the parallels between Abimelech and Absalom?

Questions for Further Study and Discussion on Judges chapters 1—9.

1. Analyze the reasons why Israel failed lamentably to drive out all the inhabitants of Palestine. See **1.34***ff.*, **1.19**, **1.25**, **1.28**, **1.33**.
2. How can Jael's deception (**4.18**) be justified—if at all?
3. Consider ch. **5** and discuss in what ways we are involved in difficult situations because of the past failures of God's people. Also what difficulties may we be creating for our successors?
4. What can we learn from the dealings of the Spirit of God with Gideon to help us understand His work in the life of a believer?
5. What unchanging principles of victory in the warfare with God's enemies are emphasized by the experience of Gideon?
6. "The sins of the Church are seldom the active doing of evil, but normally the cowardly acquiescence in evil already done." Discuss this in the light of chs. **8, 9.**

Judges 10.1—11.28

It is today widely believed that those judges of whom next to nothing is told—*viz.*, **10.1**—**5**, **12.8**—**15**—were those whose duty it was to know and recite the law at the great political meetings of Israel, when the tribal alliance met at the central sanctuary to carry out its business, mainly judicial.

At this point Israel's religion had reached its lowest point until the reign of Manasseh (2 Kings 21.1—9). The debasing of Jehovah, and the honouring of other gods beside Him, led to positive idolatry, which was not entirely cleared up until the reforms of Samuel (1 Sam. 7.3,4). To the growing pressure of the Philistines, to which the story of Samson will introduce us, there was suddenly added the much heavier and doubtless cruder oppression of the Ammonites (10.7—9). Apparently it was only then that they realized what the eighteen years of Ammonite overlordship in Trans-Jordan had meant. Even then it was left to the latter to do the fighting, when the Ammonites heard that their serfs were stirring once more.

So far as we are able to reconstruct the old Israelite marriage laws and customs, Jephthah was a fully legitimate son of Gilead, because he had been legally accepted by his father (11.1). In the lawlessness of the time he was not able to establish his rights after his father's death, and so became a bandit chief in the wilder parts of Trans-Jordan. In their moment of despair the men who had been so unjust to him had to eat humble pie and beg the terrible bandit chief to come to their help. They had to drink the cup of humiliation to the dregs and accept Jephthah virtually as a local king. "Leader" (11) is the word used in 1 Sam. 9.16, 10.1, where it is translated misleadingly "prince". The agreement was solemnly ratified at Mizpah (17).

With all its barbarity the ancient world had more concept of international right than is often the case today; war needed justification (12). Ammon conveniently forgot the real history of the area. Whether it had ever belonged to them, we do not know. If so, it had been taken by the Moabites, from whom Sihon wrested it (Num. 21.26—30). In any case, their having made no move for three hundred years made their claim invalid (26). Many have taken offence at Jephthah's speaking of *Chemosh* (24) as though he really existed. Why should a bandit chief have a better theology than his contemporaries?

Judges 11.29—12.15

Contrary to wide-spread opinion, human sacrifice was not common in the Near East at this time, nor probably at any time from 2500 B.C. on. Therefore, when it was brought, it was on occasions of outstanding importance. Jephthah knew that if Israel lost the battle, it would be the end of Israelite rule, in Trans-Jordan at any rate. So he was prepared to buy victory at the highest price he could pay. Secretly, in spite of v. 35, he must have realized the strong possibility that it would be his daughter. Every attempt to prove that Jephthah

34

did not keep his vow is valueless (39). If you think that no priest would have carried out the sacrifice, re-read **10.6**. The corruption of idolatry cannot be eliminated overnight. In that barbarous and cruel time the mourning (38,40) was not for her premature death, but because she had been unable to fulfil her function as a mother.

There seems to have been something pathological about the pride of Ephraim. They did not rise against Moab until Ehud had borne the brunt of the day (3.27); they did not stir against the Midianites until Gideon had broken their power (7.24); they ignored the needs of Trans-Jordan for 18 years until Jephthah had won a decisive victory. Though they were the strongest tribe, only the minor judge Abdon (12.15) came from them. Now they turned on Jephthah, but received no smooth words from that grim and embittered man. There followed a decisive defeat, which along with those of 1 Samuel 4.2,10 changed the history of Israel. Without them Ephraim would never have agreed to a non-Ephraimite king, but none of the other tribes would have agreed to an Ephraimite one.

It is a very strange fact that even in our own days people living in what was then Mount Ephraim suffer from the same defect of speech. It suggests that probably many of the so-called Arabs of Palestine are in fact descendants of the old tribes, who have long ago forgotten their identity as they have changed their religion.

The Bible warns us against rash promises to God, or for that matter to man. Obviously Jephthah should not have made his promise, and yet he had a higher regard for God than many who think that their promises are just like pie-crusts. A true priest would have shown him the right way, which would not have been a simple cancelling of the promise.

Judges 13

The strangest figure among the Judges is Samson. His story simply cries out for an allegorization the text will not stand. We automatically protest that such a man could not have been chosen by God. Probably many an Israelite felt the same way; this is probably the reason why the angel appeared before his birth, and why he wore the long hair of a Nazirite (5), though we gain the impression that this may have been the only part of the Nazirite vow he kept (Num. 6.2—8).

The Philistines moved south with the "sea peoples" to attack Egypt by land and sea (between 1200 and 1190 B.C.). They were completely defeated, and apparently placed by Rameses III in the area we associate with them, to guard the desert approach to Egypt. There

35

they were a military elite in the midst of a predominantly Canaanite population, whose language they quickly adopted. They gradually extended their power, first for Egypt's benefit, and then, as Egypt grew weaker, for their own. They evidently acted with wisdom and moderation, for although by Samson's time they were in unquestioned control of Judah (15.11), there seems to have been no outcry. If God had not acted, Philistine influence would have spread to such a degree that it could hardly have been eliminated. Since Israel was not yet prepared to fight for his freedom, God raised up a man with a private grievance, whose killing of Philistines did not involve his people. Since they were a military elite, their death mattered more than that of the rank and file of their forces.

As with Gideon, Manoah and his wife did not know they had to do with an angel until they saw the miracle, though his wife had some suspicion (6). It is quite probable that Manoah suspected the genuineness of the message, but blessings on his wife for a breath of sound common sense (23).

There has almost certainly never been another Samson among the people of God, but there have been many other strange characters. We are very unwilling to learn that God wants to use all the gifts He has given, while we should like to confine Him to our respectabilities. We are accustomed to hear of the unusual on the mission field, but find it hard to make room for it at home.

Judges 14

"At Timnah he saw one of the daughters of the Philistines" (1). The story begins as naturally as all that. A young man goes through the spring landscape with his parents, in his eyes the light of love. His heart urges his feet faster than his parents can or wish to go, so he is here and there, seeing what there is to see. A lion in the first fullness of his strength is nothing to Samson in his present mood, but as he rejoins his parents, he remembers what an embarrassment his unwonted strength can be to them, so he is quiet about the encounter. Evidently Manoah is well-to-do. While the young couple talk, the parents haggle, until the clink of silver outweighs the voice of racial pride. A little later they come down for the wedding, dressed in their best, and Samson idly goes to have a look at his lion, and is met by bees. There is plenty of time before the wedding feast, so he shares out the honey. Life is very sweet.

At the wedding feast the guests begin to make fun of the country bumpkin from the hills, and their tongues are sharper than the bees' stings, so he silences them with a riddle. Every spare moment in the feasting a solution is offered, each one wilder than the last, until, when the third evening of the wedding week is past, the screw is put on the bride, and she puts it on Samson. With a shock he realizes that you do marry your wife's relations. Hoping against hope he tells her the answer, but it is no shock as they gather for the last instalment of the feast to be told the answer.

In wild anger he left the house and ran at top speed the twenty-three miles to Ashkelon. The first thirty decently dressed men he could lay hold of he killed and early in the morning staggered in with his arms full of clothes. He flung them at the feet of the terrified guests and made off for home. "That's what comes of marrying your daughter to an Israelite" was the general verdict; to stop the bride's tears she was hurriedly married to the best man. Unfortunately they forgot that Samson was in love.

Judges 15.1—16.3

The fiercer the anger the sooner it cools. Love begins its work again, and Samson is going downhill happily with a kid to pacify his abandoned wife. He soon finds, however, that there is no wife and only the offer of a chit of a girl who leaves him cold. Revenge is sweet, however. With a Rabelaisian imagination he snares three hundred foxes. As the sun goes down, he ties them tail to tail with a lighted torch between. The maddened animals scatter far and wide, and all is tinder dry. Peace steals over the strong man as he sees the Philistine grain and olive trees go up in flames. He would have let the matter end there, but God had other purposes.

An inquest next morning on the damage soon established the cause, and summary injustice was done to the Philistine and his daughter. This was serious. After all, up till then it had been a family quarrel, but now his wife had been murdered, so Samson inflicted summary justice and retired to let things blow over (8). The Philistines would have done well to let sleeping dogs lie, but they decided that the master-race could not stomach an insult like that. The pique of the Judeans (11) showed that they regarded the whole matter as an inconvenient private quarrel. As Samson stood free before the Philistines, he looked round for a weapon and saw the jaw-bone of a donkey newly dead. With all its teeth in place it formed a terrible weapon. By the time the fight was over, the ground was littered with dead Philistines. A natural spring suddenly broke out, not one from the jawbone. The misunderstanding came from the fact that the place was called after the famous jawbone (*lehi*).

There is no evidence that Samson went on killing Philistines. He was satisfied, and they probably decided to leave well alone. But it was insulting, when he apparently put his head into a noose by going to Gaza, and infuriating to find one's town gates ornamenting a hillside deep in Judean territory. That story must have been told and retold in every inn from Thebes to Babylon. Doubtless this was not the only trick he played. So injured honour demanded he must be eliminated.

Judges 16.4–31

The closing scenes in Samson's life could well have been greatly misunderstood. The valley of Sorek was in the debatable land between Israel and the Philistines. Delilah could have been entirely respectable, quite possibly a widow; she was almost certainly an Israelite, otherwise they would not have offered her the enormous bribe of 5,500 shekels (5)—thirty shekels was considered to be the value of a slave. There are no reasons for thinking that Samson did not marry Delilah. If we are in a hurry to condemn her, let us ask ourselves, whether there is not a price, which need not be in money, which might make *us* disloyal.

The cause of Samson's downfall was self-confidence. He cannot have been unaware that Delilah was plotting, though he was probably far from guessing the full truth. His attitude, when his head had been shaved, shows that his strength had never been merely a natural one, but was the special gift of the Spirit.

He had dishonoured the Philistines, now they would dishonour him. Grinding at the mill was the work of the women, above all the slave-women (*cf.* Exod. **11.**5, Isa. **47.**2). Now he must play blind man's buff in grim earnest to the honour of their god (25). That to the very last it was a personal quarrel between Samson and the Philistines is seen in his final prayer. He would die with his honour at least partially saved.

Palestine at the time did not know the arch, and only from Lebanon could timber long enough to span a large hall be brought. So shorter lengths were laid from wall to pillar, and pillar to pillar On softer ground, as in the coastal plain, the pillars stood on large, flat stones to prevent their sinking in the soil. Samson's exploit lay in shifting the pillars off their supports, with the resultant collapse of the roof. It will have been at least a generation before the Philistines felt strong enough once more to attack Israel (1 Sam. **4.**1). The veteran warriors who perished in the ruins of the house of Dagon could not be so easily replaced. As we stand at the tombs of Jephthah and Samson, we may well think, "two extraordinary men!", but without them how different would the future history of Israel have been, if indeed there had been any!

Judges 17

Here we pass over to a picture of what life was really like. The story could be later than the time of Samson, but is probably earlier.

A woman, finding that someone has stolen 1,100 shekels from her, utters such blood-chilling curses on the thief that her son finds he cannot sleep at night and owns up. At the time a curse was looked on as a sort of wild animal to be let loose on the trail of the evil-doer. All she could do was to let loose an even stronger blessing that would overtake and destroy the curse (2), though we gain the impression that she was better at cursing than blessing. To reinforce the blessing the mother consecrated the silver to Jehovah, but then decided that He ought to be satisfied with two-elevenths of it (though perhaps another eleventh went on the rest of the shrine). We may judge that the graven and molten image both refer to the same thing, a bull image (Exod. 32.4, 1 Kings 12.28—in both cases a young bull rather than a calf is meant) to serve as throne for the invisible god. What use is a perfectly good shrine without a priest? A son had to serve for the time being, until a wandering Levite turned up. Levites were many, jobs few, and Micah, for the time, rich. So he was willing to become priest for the family for a good wage, board and lodging, and a new suit each year. As for Micah, he was in the seventh heaven with delight. "Now I know that the Lord will prosper me, because I have a Levite as priest" (13). The curse was dead and buried.

We may well wonder what such a family is looking for on the pages of Scripture, until we remember that this is merely a picture of what was. How much better, however, are our own times? It would be interesting to know how much church furniture, how many church buildings, have been an effort to bribe God with part, maybe a generous part, of ill-gotten gains. There is many a church and many a service where it would cause embarrassment if we asked, "Why is this here? Why do you do that?" Some might even suggest unkindly that "God's call" seems at times strangely linked with higher salaries.

Judges 18

The self-willed individual is often merely a representative of a self-willed society. Before we blame the tribe of Dan for seeking fresh fields, we should ask ourselves how much help they had received from the other tribes. Their fault lay in asking neither the other tribes nor God. The enquiry through the Levite (5) was made merely because the opportunity was handy. If it is objected that this (6) could not have been the voice of God, the answer is that if God had treated the Church as it deserved, there would be no Church.

It is not surprising that the five spies were enchanted with what they saw (9,10). Dan lies in what is perhaps the loveliest part of Palestine. Then, while the main roads passed through their portion in the coastal plain, there has never been more than a secondary road past Dan. They passed out of fighting and out of history. The five did not realize that the oracle of encouragement had been the voice of grace. They thought that the Levite's cultic collection was particularly potent, so they decided to take it along (14), as though God could be forced to go from place to place. Micah had forgotten, when he engaged the Levite, that a man who sells himself will always sell himself to a higher bidder, if the opportunity offers (20).

The Danites were a good-humoured lot. So long as they had their own way they had no grudge against the Ephraimites. No one was hurt, no house burnt down, the Levite came of his own free will, and Micah—? They needed the shrine more than he did, so what about it? No wonder Samuel had to begin by judging the people (1 Sam. 7.6) before God gave the victory. All concepts of inter-tribal responsibility had vanished. The possibility of justice at Shiloh was virtually forgotten.

At the end of the story the carefully preserved anonymity of the Levite is removed (30). He is seen as a descendant of Moses (probably not all links in the genealogy are given). The reading "Manasseh", which is found in the A.V. (K.J.V.), is due to a deliberate modification of the Hebrew text, by which the reader is invited to say Manasseh. The rabbis said, Even Moses had bad descendants; why should that be held against him? Under Jeroboam Dan graduated from a silver bull to a golden one (1 Kings 12.29).

Judges 19.1—20.11

That this story is almost certainly older than chs. 17,18 is shown by 20.28. There is also much more respect for inter-tribal justice.

Because we have become civilized, and most of us can forget what the natural man can do, at least if we stop reading the crime news, this chapter shocks us far more than does the previous story. For the Bible this is merely a story of natural man in his cruelty, self-preservation, and sensuality; the unfaithfulness to God and the ignoring of His revealed will shown in the former story were far more reprehensible.

Reading between the lines, it is fairly easy to reconstruct the background of chs. **19—21**. Benjamin, for reasons that are never hinted at, decided to leave Israel's religious alliance. That is why the Levite was treated as a foreigner to whom the men of Gibeah owed neither hospitality (**19**.15), nor security (**19**.22—25). The Levite summoned an emergency meeting of the alliance (**19**.29) to claim justice. By the refusal of the Benjaminites to carry out their alliance obligations (**20**.13), the other tribes found themselves in the same position as did the United States of America, when the slave states wished to secede. The constitution made no provision for this, so the only way out seemed to be war.

The Levite's wife is called a concubine (**19**.1), probably because she had no dowry. It was obviously a regular marriage. The urging of hospitality by his father-in-law is typically oriental. It shows why Rebekah was in such unmaidenly haste to go (Gen. 24.54—58). The attitude of the servant towards Jebus (**19**.11) shows that Jerusalem was fairly careful to remain on good terms with those who passed by. There may have been an inn in Jerusalem, but Gibeah was too small for one. They were uncommon in small places, and the rendering "inn" in Luke 2.7 must be regarded for this reason with suspicion (*cf.* N.E.B.). It is difficult to judge actions among people whose whole standard of values is different. For us the old man's suggestion was abominable (**19**.24), but for him his duties as host had to come first— he had to protect his guest. Equally the Levite had to see to it that his host came to no harm. The Levite's version puts him in a better light than he deserved (**20**.4,5).

Judges 20.12—48

The first mistake made by Israel was to accept the Levite's testimony without hearing the other side (4—7). No man can be relied on to give the whole truth in his own case. Then they passed sentence without hearing the defence (8—11). Then they bound themselves by a rash oath, even before Benjamin had a possibility of accepting their point of view. Next they expected Benjamin to accept the charge and verdict, though they had not been present when it was passed (12,13).

41

Finally they first made up their minds that it must be war, and only then did they ask God how it was to be waged (18). They gave God no chance to suggest another solution. Sorrow in the Christian life comes often from the prayer for God's guidance on the path of our own choosing.

Benjamin was obviously in the wrong and punishment had to come to them. But behind Benjamin's wrong lay also the sins of Israel, and so judgment had to begin there. Judah's selfishness over Jerusalem (see note on 1.8) led to their bearing the brunt of the first day's defeat (18). All the tribes were to blame that a considerable portion of Benjamin's territory was Canaanite (Josh. 9), and so their turn had to come the next day. Above all, however, they were to blame that they had put a portion of God's people in the ban. It is the end of this chapter that should sicken us far more than the story of Gibeah.

If God put the people of Canaan and later the Amalekites (1 Sam. 15.3) in the ban, He did so in His wisdom and patience—Canaan had waited since the time of Abraham (Gen. 15.13—16), the Amalekites from the time of the Exodus (Exod. 17.14). Even when God acted directly, He gave the contemporaries of Noah warning, all the time the ark was in building, and the cities of the plain the years of Lot's living among them. Here, however, Israel assumed that because Benjamin had separated itself from the people of God, therefore it had separated itself from God; because Israel had put Benjamin in the ban, God had too. We have here virtually a prophecy of the many bloody pages in Church history where "heretics" were annihilated to the glory of God. The one real difference is that Israel repented (21.2,3), but the persecuting Church did not.

Judges 21

Israel had sown the wind and was now reaping the whirlwind, but even so had not learnt. One may admire them for sticking to their word; one would admire them more, if they had laid their predicament before God. But even at this late stage, there seems to have been no realization of their folly. If things had gone wrong, God was to blame (15). Repeatedly we imagine that we know the will of God and set out to do it with boundless self-confidence. Then, when things go awry, we feel that God has let us down.

With typical human logic they try to cure the effects of blood-letting by further blood-letting (8—12). We need feel less sympathy with Jabesh Gilead, because, like Meroz (5.23), it knew the risks it was running. But even when we grant this, it is only a demonstration

42

of the folly of human wisdom. The later links between Jabesh Gilead and Benjamin are surely a pure coincidence (1 Sam. 11.1—11; 31.11—13).

The book of Judges ends with a scene that would belong better to a pantomime or slapstick film than the real life of the Bible. The elders of Israel stage a glorious "let's pretend" to prevent their technically breaking their promise. Four times over the author assures us (17.6; 18.1; 19.1; 21.25) that there was then no king in Israel. God had given them a political system, which in its three stages of local government, tribal unity, and inter-tribal justice and common action based on a loyalty to the one God, was almost ideal, especially under the conditions then existing. But the loyalty to God was short-lived, and even while it existed (chs. 19—21), it was purely fleshly, a keeping of the letter of the law. Once that went, the whole system began to dissolve. No one reading *Judges* can doubt that the monarchy was preferable to the chaos which then was, and yet the monarchy represented spiritually a major fall. This is a point that we need to take seriously. Some are proud, it may be rightly, of the purity and Scripturalness of our church order. But when we compare the life of our community with that of one on whom we look down, we all too often find there is more Scriptural order among those we affect to despise than in our chaos.

Questions for Further Study and Discussion on Judges chapters 10—21.

1. "A true priest would have shown Jephthah the right way, which would not have been a simple cancelling of the promise." What might this "right way" have been? Has it anything to teach us?
2. Was Samson's silence (14.9) based on humility, or due to an awareness of having violated his Nazirite vow? Was this the "thin edge of the wedge" that was to lead in due course to a far more serious violation of his vow?
3. Summarize the lessons which Samson's experience teaches us in the matter of Christian living today.
4. Why was Israel twice defeated (ch. 20)? Was the third campaign against Benjamin pressed home too ruthlessly?
5. How do the latter chapters of Judges illustrate the principle that "sorrow in the Christian life comes often from the prayer for God's guidance on the path that we have already chosen"?

Ruth 1

Ruth seems to throw a gleam of sunlight backwards over the dark pages of *Judges* and to show that the humble virtues could flourish even then. Such is not its real purpose, for in the Hebrew Bible it stands among the Writings, separated from *Judges*. It was doubtless written to show how a Moabitess figured in the genealogy of the great king David, and possibly to plead for a hand of welcome to those who came to Israel from outside.

Rainfall was very uneven in times of drought (Amos 4.7,8), and so Moab might occasionally have more rain than Bethlehem, but the move and a ten years' sojourn (4) point to a desperately poor family, for whom emigration could not worsen their lot. It follows that Orpah and Ruth must also have come from poor families, probably without dowries. By marriage they became members of the Elimelech family, and death did not release them from that fact. Naomi had, as head of the family, a legal claim over them, but she was equally under obligation to find them husbands, hence the, to us, strange language of vs. 11—13. Had she been able to offer a good dowry with the young widows, it would have been different; instead she gave them their freedom.

Ruth is not explained to us. It is easy to read more than we should into "and your God (shall be) my God" (16). By her marriage she was under obligation, outwardly at least, to serve Jehovah, and that obligation became stronger once she went to His land. Was she merely expressing this? In all probability through Mahlon and his family she had come to serve Jehovah because she wanted to. It is clear that both the widows had come to love Naomi, and there may have been a stirring of sacrificial love in Ruth's heart that made it impossible for her to leave the pitiful widow. We shall probably do best if we look on her as one of those little ones whom Jesus held up as an example to His followers.

At a time when one of the few excitements of life was a pilgrim feast or an enemy raid, and under circumstances where Elimelech's house and field must have been carefully looked after by near relatives, there is nothing surprising in Naomi's being quickly recognized (19). In fact Naomi was bringing back with her far greater riches than she realized.

Ruth 2

The fields of Bethlehem lie at various levels, and so the grain does not ripen all at once, and the harvest period (23) could last some time. Ruth was exercising her right in going to glean (Lev. **19**.9,10; **23**.22), but especially in a time like hers much would depend on how it was interpreted. When she started, one large field, divided into strips among various owners, was being reaped. She was working in Boaz' section, when he came. It looks as though it was a case of "like master like man"; the friendly answer of the head servant had kept her in that section.

Ruth need not have been surprised that Boaz knew about her (10). The men of Elimelech's clan must have been very interested in Naomi's return, for there was property involved; but harvest and the slow pace of the east ensured that no immediate steps would be taken by anyone. "Keep close to my maidens" (8): first came the men with the sickles, then the "maidens" to make the sheaves, and finally the gleaners.

"An ephah of barley" (17)—*i.e.*, just under a bushel. This shows a side of Ruth's character we often overlook. To glean that amount in a day meant, even allowing for the extras (15,16), an extraordinarily hard day's work in great heat. She was not allowing her mother-in-law to starve, if she could prevent it. That she could bring home that amount and also have a bit of her lunch left over (18) immediately showed Naomi that her treatment had been exceptional. She suspected that unexpected developments might be round the corner, but for the time being she kept her thoughts to herself.

Ruth 3,4

In a land with strict segregation of the sexes a private conversation between a man and a woman, especially if she was young, like Ruth, was almost impossible without destroying her reputation, and his too (*cf.* John 4.27). On this night, with the joy of a good harvest in his heart, Boaz was quite exceptionally sleeping out of doors; for all we know, it may have been to guard against thieves—in any case Naomi knew the local customs. Ruth bared his feet, for there was no more effective way of waking him quietly without a start than by letting his feet grow cold. When he did wake, in the moonlight he saw a woman lying there quietly. We must picture a conversation carried on in mere whispers, after which Ruth could slip away quietly, none knowing that she had been there. "Spread your skirt over your maid-servant" (3.9): to this day, in some Arab clans, a man will show that he claims a woman as wife as of right by passing the skirt of his robe round her.

45

In what follows we are not dealing with Levirate marriage (Deut. 25.5—10, Matt. 22.23—28). There is no evidence that this was ever, under any circumstances, extended from a brother to the next of kin. Further, Boaz' words (3.10) show that, whatever her duty to Naomi, Ruth was under no obligation to him. She could have tried to catch a young man by her beauty. The clue is given by the next of kin's objection (4.6); he was afraid of impairing his own inheritance. He really came into the picture because he had a pre-emptive right to buy the ground (Lev. 25.25), so there was no point in anyone else's doing it, until he knew whether the right would be exercised.

Clearly Naomi's bit of land can have had little cash value. In the understanding of an age more merciful in many things than ours its price was board and lodging so long as she lived. At her age it seemed a bargain until the next of kin realized that it also included the care of Ruth, who might easily outlive him. The question of marriage was altogether another. At that time it was understood that a woman had a right to children; if a young woman came to live in a house in any capacity she would in due course become the wife of the head of the house or of one of his sons. Quite clearly the part about perpetuating the name of the dead (4.10) was more pious talk than reality, for the genealogy of David is always reckoned through Boaz and not through Elimelech and Mahlon.

"Boaz went up to the gate" (4.1): it was only the exceptionally large city like Jerusalem that had more than one gate. So the early riser could be sure of catching anyone he wanted, as he went out to work in the fields.

Questions for Further Study and Discussion on the book of Ruth.
1. What evidence is there in this book that Boaz was a genuine man of humble faith in God?
2. In what sense does Boaz reflect and exemplify the Person and work of Jesus Christ?
3. Analyse the various forms which human love and mutual responsibility take in the book of Ruth.

1 and 2 Samuel

INTRODUCTION

Samuel, one book in Hebrew manuscripts, though divided in printed Bibles, may have received its name because Samuel is the first great character in it, or more likely because he first gave the impulse to this type of prophetic historical writing. The author—we might better say editor—has shown how the book is to be divided by his use of summaries at the end of sections. Following these indications we have:—

A.	The Book of Samuel	1 Sam. 1—7
B.	The Institution of the Monarchy	1 Sam. 8—12
C.	The Book of Saul	1 Sam. 13,14
D.	The Book of David the King	1 Sam. 15—2 Sam. 8
E.	The Book of David the Man	2 Sam. 9—20
F.	Appendix	2 Sam. 21—24

Section E, which was written by a contemporary, really ends with 1 Kings 2. The striking differences between R.S.V. and A.V. (K.J.V.) are more often than not due to the very difficult text of the Hebrew. R.S.V. often follows the early Greek translation.

1 Samuel 1

Elkanah was a Levite (1 Chron. **6.**19—28, 33—38, *cf.* 1 Sam. **8.**2). He is called an Ephraimite because of his home—*cf.* Judg. **17.**7. V.3 does not mean he ignored two of the three pilgrim feasts, but that this was a special family sacrifice (*cf.* **20.**28,29). It is probable that the number of portions was a ritually fixed matter leaving Elkanah no choice. We have only gradually mastered the art of reading and praying without speaking aloud. Hannah's bitterness enabled her to pray within herself, but her lips still moved (12,13), something Eli had previously always linked with drunkenness.

Hannah's prayer must not be regarded merely as a natural desire for a child, but must be interpreted in the light of **2.**1—10. It is widely held that mothers in Israel wanted sons in the hope of being an ancestress of the Messiah. We gain the impression that it was rather their deep passion to fulfil the functions for which they were made, and Hannah's thanksgiving supports this. If God has given us gifts, it is normal that they should be used. If they were not used, it was regarded as a reversal of the Divine order. This was, of course, before the N.T. revelation of the possible sacrifice of self to achieve the Divine purpose.

"When she had weaned him" (24): with us it is the exceptional baby that is not weaned by nine months. In the Near East a boy may not be fully weaned till three years old, and there are numerous special cases recorded where he was not weaned till five. So we may be certain that the pictures which show Hannah pushing a babe-in-arms into Eli's embarrassed arms are wrong. By the time he was taken to Shiloh he was a boy who could well fit into Eli's household.

We would think that Hannah had done more than enough to show her gratitude, but she brought a handsome thank offering with her as well. In her prayer she spoke of giving Samuel to God (11); now she is lending him (28). She was not holding back something she had promised, but she had come to know God better. She now knew that such giving could never break the link between parents and child. This she symbolized by her annual gift of a robe (2.19); he was still enfolded in his mother's love.

1 Samuel 2

Much in our modern educational systems has a sociological rather than educational motivation. It is felt that the best should come to the top irrespective of the parents' position and money. In an ideal society this would be so. Apart from v. 5, there is nothing in Hannah's song that has any obvious bearing on her case, but it is not Samuel she is thanking God for. She is overjoyed that in her God has demonstrated that principle of righteousness by which the injustices of life are checked and its wrongs reversed. Her own disability had created in her a passion for the vindication of God's purposes. This song served Mary as a pattern, when it was her turn to praise God (Luke 1.46—55).

The actions of Hophni and Phinehas are seen in all their darkness, when we remember that in every ritualistic religion the details of the ritual are seen as at least as important as the personal sanctity of the priest. By their ignoring of ritual—even if it seemed unimportant—they showed their complete contempt for God. As might be expected, there was soon contempt for the moral law as well (22).

Eli was of the family of Ithamar, not of Eleazar (*cf.* 1 Chron. **24**.3; **6**.4—10). Trustworthy Samaritan tradition claims that Eli had secured the high-priesthood because of the youth of the rightful heir in the family of Eleazar. If this is so, it aggravates the guilt of his weakness with his own sons and helps to explain the drastic punishment prophesied here (27—36) and in **3**.11—14. Note that in *Chronicles* the genealogy of Eli is passed over in silence; it can only be inferred. We can trace some of the steps by which the judgment of God was carried out: the death of Hophni and Phinehas (**4**.11), the murder of the priests at Nob (**22**.11—19) and finally the banishment of Abiathar (1 Kings **2**.26,27).

Ritual in itself is fundamentally unimportant. By the infringement in v. 13 there was no guarantee that they would get more than their share, and in v. 15 it was mainly a question of throwing their weight about. Such infringement is like rudeness. When this comes of ignorance, the wise man will overlook it. When it is deliberate, it springs from moral corruption. So it was with these young priests. Eli rebuked them for their immorality but overlooked that their disrespect to God was really something worse.

1 Samuel 3

If we think back to the days of Abimelech, Jephthah, and Samson, we need hardly be surprised that the prophetic voice was seldom heard. In such a period none would think much of it that a Levite was allowed to sleep in the temple (2). The going-out of the lamp need not point to carelessness. Exod. **27**.21, Lev. **24**.2,3 imply that the lamp did not burn by day. So the mention of the lamp may mean simply that it was quite dark.

We are apt to think that the voice of God is so clear and distinct that it cannot be confounded with any other. This can be far from the truth, so the boy Samuel has to learn his first lesson as prophet. The message was not needed by Eli; he had been told more than that. But he was a great enough man, with all his weaknesses, to let Samuel know that he had heard aright. It was also God's way of letting Eli know that he must give Samuel his chance to act as a prophet, whenever God chose to speak. In addition, because Eli was a kindly old man, Samuel found it easier to take the first step in passing on a message that was very hard to deliver.

"The Lord . . . stood forth" (10): the picture seems to be of God's coming from His cherub throne behind the veil to Samuel in the holy place. "Samuel lay until morning" (15): in the light of vs. 5,6,9, it seems clear enough that it meant that he went to sleep again. That was as it should be. The voice of God should transform life and yet so mingle with it as to let it continue its normal tenor. "Let none of his words fall to the ground" (19)—*i.e.*, God did not allow any of them to go unfulfilled. There is always a measure of contingency in prophecy, varying from case to case (*cf.* Jer. **18**.1—10). Samuel was to become virtually a second Moses, so God was careful to build up his reputation by not giving him messages the outcome of which might be changed by repentance.

Do we give God a chance of speaking to us, or would He have to wake us up to do it? Do we even want Him to speak to us?

1 Samuel 4

The Greek has an indubitably correct insertion in v. 1 showing that the campaign was started by the Philistines. They had recovered from their losses under Samson and were out to conquer the whole land. The first battle was perhaps the worst defeat suffered until then by Israel. They decided that God had left them in the lurch. It did not seem to occur to them that it might be due to their sin, nor are we told that any greeted Hophni and Phinehas as birds of ill omen when they came with their sins into the camp (4). Their idea was that God should be *forced* to fight for them. If He was not willing to do it for their sake, He would have to do it for His honour's sake. We do not do this quite so grossly, but the equivalent is not unknown among us. In the sequel God was to show that He was perfectly well able to look after the ark and His honour, but He was not going to be bullied by His people. Probably wrong confidence was linked with cowardice; possibly the unexplained reference in Psalm **78**.9 is to this battle (*cf.* **60**,**67**).

The tragedy of Eli was that he was a man of greater spiritual perception than execution. He knew well enough that the fetching of the ark was a spiritual error, and he could expect no good from his sons' having to accompany it. Jeremiah **7**.12,14, **26**.6,9 tell us of the end of Shiloh. Excavations have shown, what in any case might have been assumed, that it was destroyed at this time. The Philistines will have marched straight there and burnt the temple, not out of wantonness, but because it was the outward symbol of Israel's unity. Apparently there was just time to rescue the most sacred objects—*cf.* 2 Chron. **1**.3,5. The remainder of the priests moved to Nob (1 Sam. **21**.1—6, **22**.9,10,18,19). So Israel was left without even the outward symbols of a unity that had almost completely disappeared.

The story of Phinehas' wife (19—22) is one of the most touching in

50

the Bible, but she was wrong. The glory of God had indeed departed, but not because the ark of God had been captured; the ark had been captured because the glory had already departed.

1 Samuel 5.1—6.18

Once the ark had been taken to Philistia, God began to see to His honour. The adventures of Dagon (5.2—5) were secondary; they were merely a warning that the ark had better be kept from idol temples. Far more important was, as the Greek has at the end of 5.12, wherever the ark came "the land swarmed with mice" (cf. 6.5). Since O.T. Hebrew makes no distinction between the mouse and its bigger cousin the rat, we may well assume that the reference is to the latter, and that the tumours are plague boils. With one stroke God had undone the effects of the two Philistine victories. The terrible mortality made it impossible for them to follow them up. Otherwise there would have been nothing to prevent Israel's complete incorporation into Philistine territory.

The Philistine priests (6.2) were canny men; they knew that the woes of Philistia looked like cause and effect, but they knew also that there is such a thing as coincidence. So they advised the return of the ark to Jehovah with a guilt offering (6.3)—one of the indications of how close in outward form the Israelite sacrificial system was to the Canaanite. But Jehovah should be required to bring His ark home. Any self-respecting cows would at once have doubled back to their calves (6.7). In fact they protested vigorously against the constraint of God upon them (6.12).

For more than half a year the ark had been in Philistia (6.1), while Israel lay too stunned to know what would come next. Then the impossible, the incredible, happened. Impelled by an invisible power the ark came back. It is not surprising that the great stone in the field of Joshua of Beth-shemesh was shown for centuries after as the place where God began the transformation of His people's history. But something had happened. Until then the ark had been the mysterious guarantee of God's presence. The simpler and more superstitious may even have believed that God not only sat enthroned above it on the wings of the cherubs, but possibly even lived in it. But now they had seen it captured and the old respect had gone. Man would always rather have a magic instrument of some kind than the unchanging character of God.

In what ways do we today not trust God to look after His own honour?

51

1 Samuel 6.19—7.14

To many it seems impossible that God should kill seventy of the small town of Beth-shemesh, of hardly more than 3,000 inhabitants, because they looked into the ark, while the Philistines had been allowed to take it with apparent impunity (but with what a sequel!). The difference was that the Israelite knew that he did wrong, the Philistine did not. As the margin shows, the Hebrew text presents a major problem with its addition of 50,000 men; they are clearly differentiated from the 70 of Beth-shemesh. Those who explain it of those drawn by the news from the neighbourhood may be right, but we are safer in regarding it as the remains of a text which cannot be restored with certainty. For the time being the ark had to wait in safe and respectful custody in Kiriath-jearim (2).

We are frequently plagued by those who believe that revival is just round the corner, if we have only faith enough. There are times when God has to inflict deadly drought in the Church before He can bless. Samuel waited twenty years before he made his call to repentance; anything earlier would have led to the merely superficial. Three steps may be noted: right relationship with God (4); right relationship with men (6, "Samuel judged the people"); victory over the enemy (11). The victory was on the same ground as the previous defeat (4.1,2; 7.12), the name in the earlier passage being given in anticipation.

Earlier liberal writers made a great deal of vs. 13,14, pointing out that chs. 13,14 show us the Philistines in the heart of Israel, and so the story here is dismissed as valueless. Common courtesy demands that the compiler of *Samuel* be granted as much insight as his critics. Except in chs. 13,14 the fighting from now on is always in the border districts, and we nowhere find that Israelite cities have to be recaptured. The plain meaning is that the victory of Eben-ezer ended Philistine occupation, though not Philistine power.

Samuel must be regarded as the real restorer of Israel's religion. In the period from Saul to Solomon we find very little trace of any deeply corrupted religion, and even the use of the name Baal gradually dies out.

Thought: God wants you to win your first victory on the field where you have been defeated.

1 Samuel 7.15—8.22

The one thing Samuel was not permitted to do was to set up more than an interim political settlement. The mention of the four places, not very far apart, regularly visited by Samuel shows that he was not prepared to choose a new centre to replace Shiloh until the people by calling for the ark showed that they wanted a renewal of the old religious alliance. But they obviously blamed the shortcomings of the alliance and not their own, so the stop-gap system continued.

Samuel obviously hoped that his sons might follow him, but he did not allow his father's love to blind him. They had first to be tested, and they failed. The people had rejected the past; they could not trust God to raise up a successor to Samuel; anyway they wanted someone to lead their armies rather than praying down a miracle. All that remained was that they should lose their spiritual individuality and become "like all the nations" (5). This phrase forms the sting in their request. While God had fixed the priesthood in a hereditary line, He was free to choose the right man for civil leadership. This freedom they wished to abolish by introducing a hereditary king.

In their spiritual obtuseness they did not even realize that it might be taken by Samuel as a personal rejection; after all, he was approaching "retiring age". It was God they were rejecting (7), for they were refusing all that Samuel stood for. He who represents God must expect to be rejected, when God is rejected.

The Law contained no real place for a king; Deut. 17.14—20 was inadequate to fix his constitutional place. So vs. 10—17 must be regarded, not as a prophecy of what the king would do, but as a statement of what he was constitutionally entitled to. Though the people were too anxious to have a king to realize it, these powers ultimately meant the destruction of the then existing economic pattern. The social evils condemned by the prophets stemmed ultimately from these powers. It would be no use complaining then (18), for they had brought the situation on themselves. The story of the monarchy is of a continual, steady decline, which it had no power to arrest, because it was not essentially God-willed.

Questions for Further Study and Discussion on 1 Samuel chapters 1—8.
1. Consider the place and effect of prayer in family life, with special reference to 1 Samuel ch. 1.
2. How far is Hannah's song a prophecy, and Samuel's birth a pledge, of the coming of Christ?
3. What does the story of the Ark and its structure have to teach us about the place of visible symbols of God's presence among His people today (Jer. 3.16f)?
4. Study Samuel as a man of intercessory prayer (a priestly function) in 8.6, 12.19—25, Psalm 99.6, Jer. 15.1.

5. "He who represents God must expect to be rejected when God is rejected."—How does this principle work out at the present time?

1 Samuel 9.1—10.8

The story of Saul contains certain difficulties we cannot now answer with certainty. This comes partly from the compiler's having obviously used information from different sources. This section comes, clearly enough, ultimately from Saul himself. He is called "a young man" (2); by the ordinary usage of *bachur* he would not yet have been married, and this is borne out by his being fairly obviously under the guidance of the family slave. Yet apparently immediately after he becomes king he has a son who is a choice warrior (13.2). Either the earlier part of his reign has not been recorded, or the period between his first and second anointings was longer than the story suggests (*cf.* the language of 10.7).

To understand their arrival at Ramah remember that Saul and the slave had lost their way. The slave had probably heard someone speak of the seer without guessing his identity; hence the readiness to pay him a fee for his guidance (8). It would be interesting to know when the truth dawned on Saul, and what his feelings were as he was treated as the honoured guest with an enormous portion of meat in front of him (9.24).

He was anointed prince (*nagid*—9.16; 10.1). This was a purely secular title, giving him no religious rights such as the pagan kings had. We shall see some of the implications later. The signs, apart from the third, had no intrinsic importance, but were merely confirmations of Samuel's words. We should never despise God's ability to make Himself known in the everyday. For 10.2 see Jer. 31.15. It is clear that Rachel's tomb was shown at Zelzah, near Ramah, on the border between Benjamin and Ephraim. It is not important how this is to be reconciled with Gen. 35.19. If the traditional understanding is correct, Rachel was only one of many to have more than one grave attached to her in the popular mind. "A garrison of the Philistines" (10.5) is the least likely rendering of a word that may mean also "a representative of . . ." or "a pillar of . . ."—*i.e.*, a military trophy. The same ambiguity is found in 13.3. There is probably no link between 10.8 and 13.8—14, and the command is not explained.

The prophetic exercises of the group that met Saul (10.5,10) were apparently of the kind we sometimes meet today in Pentecostal circles. When they are the product of the Holy Spirit, they can have a tremendous influence on a person; and so it was with Saul (10.6). Then, as now, these phenomena could also be more an expression of a man's personality than of the Holy Spirit. Hence the surprise of many, who considered Saul was not of that type. A wiser man answered, "Who is their father?" (12)—*i.e.*, when the originator of the phenomena was the Holy Spirit, who could limit His choice of prophets? Clearly Saul's uncle, presumably Ner (14.51), had heard some rumours, perhaps that Saul had been guest of honour at Ramah, but wisely he kept silence (10.14—16).

There are some unexplained details in the drawing of the lots. Did Saul not have to draw himself (21)? Perhaps he bolted before they realized he had drawn it. It is one thing to know in private that God has chosen you; another to appear in public as the chosen. Presumably v. 25 refers back to 8.11—17. The Greek may be right with, "about a month later . . ." for the last sentence of ch. 10.

The way the story is told in 11.4, it looks as though Jabesh-Gilead had from the first placed its trust in Saul. Their vagueness in v. 3 was simply not to alert Nahash. But had Nahash not heard? Probably he had, and the raid was intended to express his derision of the new-made king. In his pride he did not think of keeping watch for what he might do. With 11.7 *cf.* Judg. 19.29; Saul's method had evidently been traditional for the summoning of an emergency meeting of the tribal alliance, which had never been forgotten. God had given Saul the heavy task of building the bridge between the traditional and the unknown future. So He linked him with the Judges by marking out through his prophesying that he had the Spirit of God, and also by the style of his first victory. But he had to go on, so his remaining victories bore another pattern. If we criticize Saul, let us remember his greatness of spirit at the first.

Thought: In an ungrateful world Jabesh-Gilead remained grateful (31.11—13).

1 Samuel 12

The honeymoon was rudely ended by Samuel. Presumably his address was given at Gilgal, when he considered that they had had enough of rejoicing.

First there is the accusation of ingratitude (1—5). The very call for a king was an expression of ingratitude towards Samuel. In addition the whole proceedings had not shown much thought for the feelings of the old judge. The mention of his sons (2) was merely to show how long he had served them. It will be a great thing for us, when we reach retiring age, compulsory or voluntary, to be able to do so with a clean sheet. Samuel can add, "The Lord is witness" (6).

Then there is the accusation of ingratitude towards God (6—12). As God had told him (8.7), Samuel made it clear that the demand for a king was only one form, and that not the worst, of a continuous ingratitude. R.S.V. wisely replaces the meaningless "Bedan" (11) with "Barak"; the difference in Hebrew is small. There is no necessary contradiction between v. 12 and 11.1; Nahash may well have been increasing his power for some time.

Thirdly we have the conditions for God's blessing under the new terms (13—18). The bringing of a thunderstorm at a time when one may occur naturally about once a century may seem childish and unworthy of the old prophet. The Israelites found it very hard to believe at one and the same time that Jehovah was God of both Nature and history. At the time they had no difficulty with Him as God of history (cf. 8,9,11), but their honouring of the Baals (10) showed their difficulty in believing that He was God of Nature also. So God's control of Nature had to be demonstrated. It was not so much that their asking for a king was wicked (17), but their asking betrayed their essential wickedness.

It is most important that we learn the lesson of v. 20. As Israel with the Gibeonites (Josh. 9), our sin may cause something to happen that was not in God's will. Instead of trying to root out that which cannot be removed, we must learn to live with it, letting it remind us of our sin, so that we walk the more closely with God. We may even find at the end that God has used the fruit of our sin for His glory and our final good.

1 Samuel 13

For many, v. 1 in R.S.V. must come as a sort of brutal challenge. The damage to the text was at first doubtless accidental, but if scribes made no attempt to find the correct figures from other MSS, it was a Spirit-inspired judgment on the reign of Saul as a whole (cf. 1 Chron. 10, where Saul's death only is recorded). Strangely enough, the other details that have come down to us are too fragmentary for us to make any valid guess at the length of Saul's reign.

Saul realized at once that the quality of a small standing army was worth more than the quantity of the militia, which was effective only for a short campaign. For Jonathan's action (3,4) see note on **10**.5. On the whole, "and the Philistines heard of it" would suit a trophy pillar best. We should follow the Greek at the end of v. 3 and render, "and the Philistines heard of it, and proclaimed, 'The Hebrews have revolted.'" "Hebrews" is the name used by foreigners (19, **14**.11); when it is the people speaking, it is "Israel" (4,20).

As remarked on **10**.8, we cannot easily link **13**.8 with it. Saul had his "army chaplain" (**14**.3,18), and there was bound to be a priest at a sanctuary as great as Gilgal. Saul was merely looking for an excuse to act as priest himself—*i.e.*, he wanted to extend his power from the civil to the religious sphere, and it was this that caused his rejection (14).

In a hilly land like Palestine it would call for a much longer and more complete control than the Philistines ever exercised to eliminate all the smiths. The sea peoples (see note on Judges **13**), including the Philistines, owed their military power largely to their use of iron rather than bronze weapons. They had been willing to sell iron agricultural implements, but not weapons, nor the "know-how" of working iron. There will have been smiths in Israel able to work the despised bronze, but not iron. The Philistine blacksmiths' charges were exorbitant: a *pim*—*i.e.*, two-thirds of a shekel—for the larger, and one-third for the smaller, articles.

Thought: *The last five minutes of waiting are often the most difficult!*

1 Samuel 14.1–46

The Philistines had marched up by the passes of Aijalon and Beth-horon, had seized part of the central ridge and had gone further east to Michmash. Here they were separated from Saul's position in Geba (*cf.* 2 with **13**.5, **14**.5) by a deep ravine. They had virtually isolated Benjamin from the centre and north. The raiders went north, east and west, but not to the south, held by Saul. The general site of Jonathan's exploit is known, but not the exact place; in any case the crossing of the ravine, even today, is difficult.

The plan was that they should go down to the ravine bottom (8). If the Philistines said they would come down to fight them, they would await their coming (9); if they were challenged to climb up on the Philistine side, they would do so (10). Once they started climbing, they would probably have been invisible to those above, so it is not clear whether the Philistines dismissed them as mad, or whether they jocularly waited until they reached the top. No sooner had the panic started, than it was continued by the earthquake (15).

The ravine was narrow enough for those at Geba to see the panic, but not to be sure of its reason. It could have been a trap, so Saul, to discover God's will, called for Ahijah and the ephod (so the Greek; quite apart from 7.2, there is no evidence that the ark was used for discovering God's will), but before it was given, the reality of the panic seemed to make it unnecessary. Saul's oath (24) belongs to those superstitions which think that God is more likely to listen if men indulge in unnecessary self-denial. If God withheld His answer (37), it was because He often takes our stupidities as seriously as we mean them. R.S.V. is wrong in suggesting that the people ate the blood (32); they ate the animals *on* the blood—*i.e.*, they made no attempt to cook them away from the blood-stained earth. R.S.V. has rightly followed the Greek in v. 41. It is unlikely that we are meant to press "so the people ransomed Jonathan" (45); if there was any price paid, it was that of an incomplete victory.

1 Samuel 14.47—15.35

These verses in ch. 14 are intended as a summary—*i.e.*, we are passing from the history of Saul to the coming of his successor. Everything told us from here on about Saul is in the light of David. Note that as a warrior Saul was very successful (see also note on 2 Sam. 1.24). "Ishvi" (49) is indubitably Ish-bosheth (2 Sam. 2.8). His name was really Esh-baal (1 Chron. 8.33, 9.39). Later scribes changed Baal to "Bosheth" (shame), but here to *yo* (from Yahweh), corrupted to *vi*. Abinadab (31.2) has accidentally dropped out. For this use of *bosheth*, *cf.* Mephibosheth with 1 Chron. 8.34, 9.40, and Jerubbesheth (2 Sam. 11.21) with Judg. 6.32.

As you will have seen from *Joshua*, the stringency with which the ban was operated varied from case to case. Here (15.3) it was as absolute as in the case of Jericho (Josh. 6.17—19) and Ai (Josh. 8.2). If this was not carried out (15,20,21), it must have been because Saul thought he understood God's will better than Samuel and informed his captains accordingly; note his genuine surprise in v. 20. Once again he was trying to assume religious rights, and so he was rejected once again. The fact that he had once "prophesied" (10.10) did not make him a greater prophet than Samuel.

Before you feel sorry for the Amalekites, remember that they had been given more than 200 years to repent. Their original sin (Exod. 17.8) had been a breach of fundamental desert law, the attempt to

58

monopolize the water supply, and doubtless they had not changed. Samuel's words to Agag (33) should be sufficient for anyone with an imagination.

Man's first sin was disobedience. It may very well be that Saul persuaded himself that Samuel had misunderstood God's will, just as the serpent persuaded Eve that God did not really mean what He had said. But whatever excuse we make for Saul, his action was as disastrous for him and his family as Eve's for mankind. Should you think that the people were carrying out God's command indirectly, for there is no reason to think that vs. 15,21 are in any way an attempted evasion by Saul, remember that most of the sacrifices would have been peace offerings, and these were for the most part eaten by the worshippers. You are not giving much to God if you will be the chief beneficiary of the gift.

1 Samuel 16

Samuel's sacrificing had been a regular part of his former activity; Saul's anointing had not changed his rights in this respect, and so he had probably continued his practice. But the breach betweeen him and the king was such public property, that the elders of Bethlehem were alarmed af his coming. They asked him, "Does your coming mean peace?" (4)—i.e., "Is it for our good?"

There was no reason why David's anointing should have been understood as an anointing as king; prophets could be anointed (1 Kings 19.16). In view of Saul's growing uneasiness and suspicion it is probably better to render not "in the midst of his brethren" (13), but "from the midst"—i.e., privately. David was not given the unnecessary outward gift of "prophecy" like Saul, but he received the inward reality of the Spirit.

For the Hebrew understanding, "an evil spirit from the Lord" (14) created a rather different impression than it does for us. With us it suggests a spirit that was morally evil, as is the case in the N.T.; here it merely conveys the thought that the outcome of his working was calamitous for Saul. It is worth noting that the accurate rendering is: "continuously tormented him". The fact that his courtiers suggested a purely natural remedy, which was successful for the time being, shows that Saul was not regarded as a case of demon possession in the N.T. sense.

The description of David as "a man of valour, a man of war" (18) virtually forces us to assume some lapse of time between his anointing and his taking up an official position at court, which we must not exaggerate in its first stages. He was appointed as "one of his armour bearers" (21).

In the light of difficulties raised by the next chapter we must stress that v. 22 creates the impression of a full-time entry into the royal service. In addition, the very painful nature of Saul's illness makes it very improbable that Saul would have permitted David to go very far from the court. It seems that the story of Goliath (see notes on ch. **17**) is earlier, but because it did not lead to an appointment at court, it is put later, as being of no special importance in the working out of the Divine purpose.

1 Samuel 17.1–54

We must look briefly at the main difficulties of this story, mainly because they are so often insisted on in schools and colleges. They are: (*a*) If David had been Saul's harper and armour-bearer, he would have had no difficulty in going direct to Saul (31); (*b*) vs. 33—36 are hardly compatible with **16**.18; (*c*) ignorance of David's identity (55—58) is hardly explicable; (*d*) David's periodic return to the work of a shepherd (15) seems unnatural.

In the Greek (*Codex Vaticanus*) **17**.12—31 and **17**.55—**18**.5 are missing. If we could accept this as correct, the problem would largely vanish; but the translator probably omitted the verses just because he saw the difficulty. If on the other hand we assume that the story is earlier than that in **16**.14—23, though probably after the anointing, then most (not all) of the difficulties vanish. We would have to see in v. 15 the effort of a late editor to explain an obvious problem. Another pointer to an earlier date for this story is the fact that no effort was made at the time to implement the promise that he should be Saul's son-in-law; if he was merely a lad, he was too young for marriage. The argument based on 2 Sam. **21**.19 is dealt with there.

The reason why the two sides faced one another harmlessly for forty days (16) was because "the valley of Elah" (2) was little more than a ravine; anyone trying to cross it in the face of the enemy would be going to almost certain death. David could do it only because he was responding to Goliath's challenge; by the rules of the contest he had to let him cross.

David expected a victory, not because he was an Israelite and Goliath a Philistine, but because he interpreted Goliath's words as a challenge to God Himself (45—47). We must always be prepared to distinguish between our cause and God's. They are not necessarily the same. But behind the confidence lay an assurance based on doing his duty. Whenever (better than "when" in v. 34) lion or bear interfered with his sheep, he dealt with them as a matter of course. We shall not do great things for God unless we learn to do the lesser as well. If God had looked after him while he did his duty, how much more when he was God's champion?

"His tent" (54)—probably God's tent, *cf.* **21**.9. "To Jerusalem": presumably David had the head pickled and hung it in his banqueting hall after he had captured Jerusalem.

1 Samuel 17.55—18.30

From this point until David settled in the Philistine country (**27**.1) it is impossible to fix the chronological connection between many of the stories. We must not assume that because two stories stand side by side the second must necessarily flow out of the first. Normally this problem will not be discussed in these comments.

Saul had been privately anointed by Samuel, so he had every reason for expecting that he would do the same to someone else, so we can easily understand his eyeing anyone rising to prominence with suspicion. So there is nothing unnatural in vs. 8,9. "He raved" (10): literally "he prophesied"; R.S.V. is, of course, correct, but it throws light on how some of the less reputable prophets behaved. "And Saul cast the spear" (11): David would not have waited for the second attempt; render "prepared to throw".

At this stage Saul still knew what he did in his fits of semi-madness, so in his fear of consequences he detached David from the court. This led only to increasing successes for David, and to his becoming steadily better known and loved throughout the country. God's hand was so obviously in it all, that "Saul stood in awe of him".

In his hope of driving David to suicidal rashness Saul remembered the promise he had made when Goliath was challenging Israel (**17**.25). Why he did not keep it, we do not know. He may have married off Merab in one of his fits of gloom. Michal's love for David rather changed the position (20), and Saul decided he had better press ahead. David's diffidence (**18**,23) must not be interpreted too literally. It did represent the poverty of David's family; David could not afford to give the king a gift of the conventional size. Far more important, however, was the compulsion David was under not to do anything that could be interpreted by Saul or his enemies as a sign of plotting.

The Philistines were the only neighbours of Israel that did not practise circumcision (*cf.* Jer. **9**.25,26). Normally, when one wanted to count the enemy dead, one cut off a hand. In this case the foreskins were a guarantee that the dead were Philistines.

Saul was a tragic figure but quite typical. He knew he had been rejected by God, but for all that he thought he could fight God's rejection.

Questions for Further Study and Discussion on 1 Samuel chapters 9—18.

1. What reasons are there that made Benjamin a suitable tribe to provide the first king?
2. Consider ch. 13: (*i*) does God specifically test an individual today? (*ii*) what is the relationship between usefulness to God and obedience to Him?
3. In what way do the excuses which Saul made (ch. 15) find expression among Christians nowadays?
4. "David was not chosen king by God because of his musical skill, but without it he might never had become king." Work out the implications of this in terms of Christian vocation.
5. Contrast the way in which Saul and David met the challenges of life. What can we learn from these?

1 Samuel 19

We are now introduced to the gradual break-up of Saul. His awe and fear first made him try to get someone else to bear the responsibility of murder (1). This is one of the corruptions of power. Saul would have claimed ignorance, while the murderer would have claimed superior orders! Next day Saul swore solemnly that David would not be put to death (6), yet a few weeks later he tried to pin him to the wall (10). That this mood was not passing madness is seen in his attempt to arrest him and his deliberate challenge to Samuel.

He was not then mad enough to flout a basic convention of Eastern life: a man must not be disturbed at night in his own house. Saul's men simply watched the door till dawn. How there came to be *teraphim* in David's house we are not told. If we accept the translation of vs. 13,16, we can hardly suggest that he was ignorant of its existence, even if, as probable, it belonged to Michal. But both Genesis 31.19,34 ("household gods"—*teraphim*), and the generally small size of religious images at the time, are against the concept of a man-sized image, which the traditional translation suggests. A more likely rendering is, "Michal took the *teraphim* and put them by the bed"

(13). In popular thought all serious illness was due to evil spirits, and the *teraphim* were placed beside the bed to guard it. The black goats-hair rug and the crumpled clothes were enough to suggest someone in the bed. Saul's complete egomania is shown by his question to Michal (17).

God gave Saul one more warning. He deliberately challenged the spiritual authority of Samuel, with whom David had sought sanctuary. A mysterious power streamed out from Samuel's prophets and immobilized Saul's soldiers, presumably in the same way as it did Saul. When Saul himself intervened, madly thinking that his kingly power was greater than the power that had made him king, he found himself helplessly walking the last few miles and then caught up in the spiritual exercises, until he lay exhausted and half naked in a trance for a day and a night. What might have been a spiritual uplift became his shame. The question once asked in surprise now became a sneer (24). The sign of God's favour had become one of God's forsaking.

1 Samuel 20

At this point we must either see chronology dislocated or understand that Saul was by now suffering from schizophrenia, and was no longer conscious of what he had done during his mad fits. Only in one way or the other can we reconcile the murderous assaults of ch. **19** with the expectation that David would be at the royal table (6,18,19,26,27). Note that Jonathan seems to have no idea of how far things had gone (2). We can see something of the nature of the time in the struggle between Jonathan's trust in David and his fears (14—17).

Saul's general mental instability is seen in vs. 24—34. Jonathan evidently acted as Royal Chamberlain, and so Saul assumed that any courtier who was absent would have cleared himself with him (27). But when he found that Jonathan had acted within his powers, he flared up in fierce anger, and ordered David's immediate arrest and execution (31). When Jonathan asked for a motive for the verdict, he was himself threatened. "Saul cast his spear" (33): see note on **18.11**. "Because his father had disgraced him" (34): obviously it had been Jonathan who had been disgraced. The insult to his mother—Saul's wife!—conforms to quite a common Oriental type, and is not really meant to involve the mother as well.

The plan of vs. 18—22, 35—41 was based on the fact that the whole of David's future might depend on his avoiding the accusation of plotting against Saul, the Lord's anointed. Had the news got round that the warning to leave the court had come from Jonathan, he would have had to flee and join David, and no one would have believed that there was not an active plot against Saul. The limits of the plot were, of course, the saving of David's life—quite another matter.

Jonathan went out with one of his pages. He told the boy to fetch any arrows he might shoot. As the boy went, he shot over his head. The boy soon reached the arrow (37), but by then he had shot two even further, so the boy had to go further still (38). When he had brought back the three arrows (20), he was sent back to the city with the bow and arrows. This should have been all (40), but David, seeing that the coast was clear, came out of hiding. Evidently the friends had a premonition that they might not see one another again.

1 Samuel 21.1—22.5

Should David have fled from Saul's court? It is more than difficult to say, but he certainly should not have done it in the way he did. He was so broken by his emotional parting from Jonathan that he went unprepared and without a plan, so everywhere he came he brought danger to himself or others.

It is difficult to evaluate the story of Ahimelech. 22.15 shows us that we do not have the whole story in vs. 1—6. The Oriental's penchant for minding other persons' business means that the conversation may in part have been intended for Doeg and anyone else who might overhear. In any case, David's plight without food and weapons shows how unplanned his flight had been.

The next step confirms the impression. There were too many widows and orphans in Gath who hated his name. In addition some may have thought it a foolhardy act of spying, for news of his final break with Saul will not have preceded him. In the very jaws of death David suddenly came to himself and pulled himself together. He had been mad to go to Gath; good, he would play the madman properly! Since it was believed that the mad had been touched by the gods, he was under their protection and was allowed to go, if he wished.

On his return to Judah, David found that the news was abroad. Immediately he was joined by his relations. With Saul in the mood he was, they had no choice (cf. his treatment of the priests, 22.18,19). Even his old parents had to be brought to safety (22.3,4). David knew that they could not stand an outlaw's life, and he may have expected that the memory of Ruth, the Moabitess, in his ancestry would make the king more willing to receive them.

Unexpectedly David found other adherents as well (22.2). There are always some who are dissatisfied, but it takes much to make a man willing to be an outlaw. Justice is more than the enforcement of the letter of the law; it is seeing that right is done. Saul had become so concerned with his fears and suspicions, that he had lost the ability to put himself into another's shoes and discover what was really right.

"The stronghold" (4,5): in the first case it probably means "so long as he was an outlaw". The second is more difficult, but probably refers to an otherwise unnamed place in Moab. "The forest of Hereth" (22.5) was probably at Horesh (23.15), south of Hebron. A forest was wild, broken land covered with scrub.

1 Samuel 22.6—23.18

The immediate effect on Saul, when the mystery of David's disappearance was cleared up, was to feel sorry for himself. There is little spiritual hope for a man in this condition, when he persuades himself that everyone is wrong except himself. Saul may have discovered about Jonathan's farewell to David, but it is more likely that the accusation is the fruit of his own guilty conscience. That Doeg had kept silence until then shows how mad Saul was capable of being. Doeg was completely devoid of scruples, but he knew that Saul was capable of flying at him in a mad rage and killing him. "All his servants" (22.6)—i.e., his courtiers.

Ahimelech knew he was treading on thin ice. He probably told Abiathar not to come with him to Saul, but to be ready to flee. That he came to David with an ephod (23.6) suggests that he had had his bag ready packed. We do not know whether it was Doeg that destroyed Nob (22.19), but if he did, he was acting on Saul's command. Treason to him was now treason to God, and those guilty had to be put in the ban.

Once again we meet David's essential planlessness. He had not asked himself how 600 men would occupy themselves doing nothing in the wilder parts of Judea. The grim realities of outlawry have little relationship to Robin Hood in the merry greenwood of Sherwood. The incursion of the Philistines (23.1) enabled David to go on building up his reputation as saviour of his people, while Keilah's position in the centre of Judah showed up Saul's decreasing ability to guard his kingdom.

We must not be too hard on Keilah for its willingness to hand over David, for it was too small to be able to resist Saul's army for long.

Unless he was prepared for full-scale civil war, to rely on Keilah was absurd. The apparent contradiction between 23.13 and 14 is probably explained by Saul's keeping a number of agents spying on David's whereabouts, but only taking action when he thought he had trapped him.

Jonathan, with a vivid sense of the strain on David, went "to strengthen his hand in God" (16). Small-minded men criticize him for not joining David. They forget that Saul was still the legal king. David neither killed him nor fought him, but only dodged him. No one had the right to leave Saul's service, till life in it was made impossible. Choice is not always as obvious as some would have us believe.

1 Samuel 23.19—24.22

We may easily excuse Keilah (23.12), but not Ziph. They had a right to demand that David move out of their territory, but not to betray him. The two geographical descriptions (19,24) place David down towards the Dead Sea ("in the Arabah", 24), southward of Ziph, on the other side of Jeshimon (*i.e.*, the Wilderness of Judea). Thanks to the treachery of the Ziphites Saul very nearly caught David (26), but God saw to it that the news of the Philistine raid came in the nick of time.

"Engedi" (23.29) is one of the very few spots in this wild area where there is constant fresh water. The description "Wildgoats' Rocks" (24.2) for the heights above Engedi is most expressive as any who have seen them will know. The very effort to move an army here was a sign of madness. For David's men the coincidence that Saul chose just their cave was sign positive that God had arranged it to give David his opportunity of revenge (4). David accepted the Divine overruling, but as an opportunity for showing his abiding loyalty. He was so great-hearted that he even regretted having put Saul to the shame of a damaged dress.

David had in these desperate days learnt the lesson that he must leave his wrongs and vindication in the hands of God. It is not easy to judge how far David was in fact telling the truth, when he put the cause of Saul's hatred on others (9; 26.19). It may have been simply politeness in seeking to minimize Saul's fault (*cf.* note on 26.19), or in fact there may have been jealous men who, seeing how the wind was blowing, kept stirring up Saul's infatuation.

As with David in Gath (21.10—15), the sudden realization of the presence of the angel of death sobered Saul for a moment. He realized that the moral greatness of David marked him out as the coming king (20). Unlike in 26.21, when the shock and the impression were less, Saul did not suggest his return to court, for he knew he could not trust himself.

How petty is Saul; how great is David! Why should David kill Saul's family, if he does not kill Saul himself? Yet Saul demands an oath from him, but offers nothing himself. Saul was not going to swear to David, for secretly he was looking forward to the next access of madness, when he could forget and try once more to kill David. "Stronghold" (22) may refer back to 23.29.

1 Samuel 25

At the time it seems to have been a special honour for a man to be buried in his house (1; *cf.* 1 Kings 2.34). For someone who did not know the story, ch. 24 ended on a note that seemed to promise reconciliation; ch. 25 begins with the knell of coming doom—the one man who could have reconciled them was dead.

Let your imagination work on the story of Nabal and Abigail. How did outlaws in Jeshimon live? There were no king's deer to shoot, as in Sherwood. We see them acting as unofficial police, protecting the region against raiders (16). But then the "insurance premium" had to be paid (6—8). Nabal could have refused politely, but he had probably already drunk too much (36), so he insulted David as well as refusing (10,11,14). David might have accepted a refusal, but injured honour had to be cured by bloodletting (13).

That Abigail could lay hands at once on such an amount of food (18), even allowing for the smaller size of the "loaves", shows the scale of the feasting and the folly of Nabal. David's answer shows that he understood the real reason behind Abigail's concern (32,33). Once human standards are allowed to dominate our thinking, there is no limit to the complications that may ensue. Human standards demanded that David avenge his honour, but had he done so, he would have had a massive blood-feud with the influential Calebite clan on his hands, and Judah would never have been able to ask him to be king. He waited; Nabal had a stroke (37), which in the popular mind was clearly an act of God, and so a vindication of David's honour. He also gained an intelligent wife (42) who allied the Calebites to him.

It must be looked on as sheer coincidence that David's third wife (43) had the same name as Saul's (14.50). The Jezreel is that of Josh. 15.56, not far from Maon and the Carmel of this story. By these two marriages David had gone a long way towards securing himself in the far south of Judah.

The previous chapter ended on a note where reconciliation was still possible; this ends with every hope gone. 2 Samuel 3.13—16 can be explained only if Saul's action in re-marrying Michal was completely illegal and invalid.

1 Samuel 26

You will know a man by the company he keeps. At their former approach to Saul (23.19) the Ziphites were probably moved by the thought of gain. Now there is some of the malignity apparent which we have seen in Saul. They were probably made jealous by David's growing influence to the south of them. David's growing safety is seen in his not trying to avoid Saul. Now it is rather David who is the cat and Saul the mouse.

Saul had probably encamped on a flat hill-top. By climbing a higher hill David could see all the details in the moonlight. Saul slept at the heart of the camp—the rendering "the place of the wagons" (5, R.V.) is impossible, for they could never have been brought there—and his men were around him. Just as at Engedi God had led Saul to David's cave, so here He had poured "deep sleep" (12) on them.

It was probably a mere impulse that sent David climbing into the camp, but once again he faced the temptation of taking his future into his own hands and triumphed over it. If we compare the two incidents, we shall see that there is a sharper edge to David's words here. The losing of Michal had wounded him deeply, and he had realized more than ever before how utterly implacable Saul really was.

Did David himself believe the words, "Go, serve other gods" (19)? Probably not, but many at the time thought that once the frontiers of Israel were crossed, one was no longer under the direct control of Jehovah, unless one was fighting for Him. We must not forget, however, that when one had left Israel, there was no possibility of public worship. The very fact that David spoke like this shows that he was already toying with the fatal idea of going to the Philistines.

Note David's courtesy even under these circumstances. He attributed Saul's actions either to God—this would call for a sacrifice by David to appease Him—or to the advice of evil men (19). He never suggested that Saul himself was the person to blame. There is on David's part a respect for the powers that be as ordained by God which we seldom meet today.

Are we really convinced that God's power is the same and shows itself the same, wherever we may be?

1 Samuel 27

The Christian's fainting fits are an element we do not always sufficiently allow for, and which, but for the grace of God, may radically damage his spiritual life. What made David go to Philistia? First of all, I imagine, sheer tiredness. To have to go on living month after month in Jeshimon will sap the finest constitution and cause the most finely tempered mind to cry out for relaxation. Then, for some at any rate, it is almost impossible to grow accustomed to the abiding presence of the angel of death. Each new threat to his life came with renewed force, with the impact of all the previous efforts behind it. Then the mounting impression of Saul's malignancy will also have had its effects. There are many on whom contact with the diabolical has a laming power. His marriages will also have made him conscious of the life he was asking his wives to lead. Then, with David we repeatedly have the impression of a man of impulse, of one who acted first and thought afterwards.

David was in quite a different position from when he first went to Achish (**21**.11). Everyone knew now that he had broken irreparably with Saul, and so there was no question of his being a spy. Then his 600 hardened men made him a most valuable mercenary captain. The worst danger he exposed himself to was being regarded in Israel as a turncoat and traitor. Deep-rooted hatred against him and his men in Gath caused him to be moved to Ziklag, a former Simeonite town (6).

A mercenary captain had to justify his existence, and that in Achish's eyes was the raiding of Israel. Instead he raided the desert tribes, probably on friendly terms with the Philistines. For "the Geshurites" (8), *cf.* Josh. **13**.2, not to be confused with the north-eastern Geshur (Josh. **13**.11). The murder of women and children during raiding, unless the ban had been laid on a people, was considered despicable and reprehensible. David had to sink to the lowest depths conceivable to hide what he had been doing (11). To that he had to add hard lying. We should not forget this side of David, with its moral degradation.

Can you say, "I waited patiently for the Lord"?

1 Samuel 28

As things went from bad to worse Nemesis suddenly overtook David. He was unexpectedly called to march with Achish against Israel. In his mental agony he used high-sounding but meaningless words (2). Achish understood them as a declaration of loyalty and made David the captain of his bodyguard. We leave David in his sore agony for Saul who was in worse.

Saul, like not a few others, had to have guidance, not out of love for God but for fear of making mistakes. When they think they know the right course, they will ask no one, but it is almost impossible to stir them when they are in doubt. That was Saul's position, when he suddenly found himself cut off from every form of guidance (6). He collapsed, though there is no evidence that he was in special danger. The change of direction of Philistine attack does not suggest an all-out attempt to break Israel, but rather an attempt to strengthen their weakening grip on the great trade route.

Saul did not turn to other gods—let that be said on his side—but to the wise and kindly old man who had first turned his feet to the paths of greatness. He hoped to get into touch with him through "a medium" (7)—a far better translation than "witch". The outcome is not an affirmation but a rejection of the truth claimed for spiritism. No one was more terrified than the medium herself (12). Whom, or what, she expected we are not told, but it was certainly not Samuel. That God permitted Samuel to return is no evidence that mediums normally have such power. All that Saul gained by flouting God's commandment was a knowledge of the future that effectively and completely lamed him. God's withholding from us of an effective knowledge of the future is one of His most gracious acts. Most of us would either break under the knowledge, as did Saul, or abuse it.

A look at a map will show you that to reach Endor from Mt. Gilboa Saul had to skirt the Philistine army at Shunem. He could easily have been killed before the battle, and it would have been better for Israel if he had been.

Why should we expect God to guide us, if we ask Him only when it suits our convenience?

1 Samuel 29

When men are at their wits' end, then God displays that the impossible to them is child's play to Him. The story goes back to before 28.4 to Aphek in the coastal plain (4.1), where the Philistine units joined and were reviewed. One more drop in the cup of David's degradation awaited him; the Philistine commanders proclaimed that he was not to be trusted. In spite of his desperate plight we may well judge that they were wrong, but David deserved it. He was in a plight like that of Sir Launcelot, of whom Tennyson wrote:

> *His honour rooted in dishonour stood,*
> *And faith unfaithful kept him falsely true.*

With grim irony the writer depicts Achish apologizing profusely to David for sending him home. He had no idea that this was David's happiest hour. David, when he realized that this was final and irrevocable, played for safety. He put on a scene and protested vigorously against the indignity done to him. Fortunately he did not overdo it, so that Achish remained without suspicion. Try to picture the scene next morning as the Philistines marched north and David and his men south. Doubtless they had to accept many a jeer and gibe they did not venture to answer. The psalm itself may have been written later in David's life, but the striking picture of Psalm 124.7 must surely have come to David that morning: "We have escaped as a bird from the snare of the fowlers; the snare is broken and we have escaped."

God gave David encouragement on his way as well. He received unexpected reinforcements, which were very soon to prove most acceptable (1 Chron. 12.19—21).

In ch. 30 we shall find how David's fortunes reached their lowest point only to mend and rise rapidly. So here is the point where you would do well to revise the story of David up to date. Try to judge what were the factors which were to make of him a king according to God's own heart. Do some of the weaknesses we meet in these years of suffering reappear later? In the account of him as king do you find earlier traits appearing? Can you think of passages in the Psalter which seem to link with his experiences in these years?

1 Samuel 30

David and his men had no premonition of evil; they could have covered the sixty miles from Aphek quicker. There is no contradiction between the mention of the Amalekites (and 27.8) and ch. 15. A numerous nomadic tribe will never be sufficiently concentrated to be wiped out in one operation. There is no suggestion that the raid was intended as revenge. The Amalekites knew that the Philistines, including David, had marched against Israel; from vs. 14,16 we see it was a general raid. The "Cherethites" were Philistines. Ziklag was less able to resist, because it did not include veteran soldiers too old to march on active service.

The extent to which David's disgraceful conduct had marred his image in the eyes of his followers is seen in their willingness to stone him (6). "David strengthened himself in the Lord his God . . ." "Bring me the ephod" (6,7): this is the first time since Judah was left that we hear such language. David had finally been brought to an end of himself, and from now on his fortunes changed.

The exhaustion (10) was due as much to the inordinate weeping (4) as to the march to and from Aphek. The lack of watch by the Amalekites was because they knew the Philistines to be far away (16). It would have been impossible to mount an effective attack in the dark. David attacked at first light and continued until dark (17). Since no other camels are mentioned, these are all that will have been available. The rehabilitation of David by his victory is shown by the spontaneous acknowledgement of the booty as his (20)—*i.e.*, everything that had not been taken from Ziklag itself. We must not be too hard on "the wicked and base fellows . . . with David" (22); they had not been set much of an example ever since David chose the downward path.

In the list of Judean cities a couple of alterations should be made. "Bethel" (27) is Bethul (Josh. **19.**4); "Aroer" (28) was east of Jordan, so read either Adadah (Josh. **15.**22), or possibly Ararah.

Those who, like David, have turned to God in their deepest distress have been repeatedly amazed at the speed with which He has been able to change their fortunes.

Thought: "My strength is made perfect in weakness."

1 Samuel 31

The choice of Mt. Gilboa for Israel's position revealed the eye of a good general. It was a position of great defensive strength, and whatever the Philistine plans, they could not ignore a force stationed there. Yet, if we are to believe the Amalekite's story, and there is no valid reason for not doing so, the Philistines used their chariots in the battle (2 Sam. **1.**6), which would have been impossible on the mountain slopes. Clearly, instead of staying in his defensive position, Saul, in his despair, marched down the slopes to ground where all the advantages were with the Philistines.

Then, as earlier, the Israelites were not able to face the chariot charge, and fled. We do not know whether Saul could not fly, or did not deign to. Probably he tried, with his crack troops around him, to slow up the flight, retreating foot by foot. He saw his three sons fall near him. To break the stubborn resistance the Philistines brought up their archers and severely wounded Saul. He did not want to share the fate of Samson, and so took his life. "All his men" (6): in the setting, clearly Saul's body-guard is meant. They remained true to him to the last.

"The other side of the valley" (7)—*i.e.*, the north side. This verse confirms the opinion expressed on **28.4** that the Philistines' purpose was to strengthen their hold on the trade route. They conquered only the southern strip of Galilee and that part of Gilead opposite Beth-shan (not even as far south as Jabesh-gilead). The view so often found in modern books that Israel lay helpless at the feet of the Philistines lacks Scriptural foundation.

Saul's body deserved better treatment, for he and his sons had fought gallantly. We should be glad that the men of Jabesh-gilead at least guaranteed him decent burial (*cf.* also 2 Sam. **21**.12—14). The modern tendency is to translate v. 12 "and they anointed them there" instead of "and burnt them there". Though quite possible, the mention of "their bones" (13) makes it improbable. Putrefaction had almost certainly set in. In addition, if the Philistines traced the bodies to Jabesh-gilead, it would be almost impossible to identify bones.

Saul took his life rather than be dishonoured, and yet his corpse was dishonoured. This points to the central weakness in his life. He was a man who had been touched by God and so could not do without God. Yet he was never willing to give unconditional trust and surrender.

Questions for Further Study and Discussion on 1 Samuel chapters 19—31.

1. What does ch. **19** teach about sacrificing love? Relate this to the cost of our love for Christ (*cf.* 1 Cor. **13**).

2. How does David's "exile" relate to Christian experience today? What special temptations beset us in times of spiritual "exile"?

3. Consider the teaching that we may draw from ch. **22** on the subject of jealousy (see also Prov. **6**.34, **27**.4, Rom. **13**.13,14).

4. What example does David give us in his behaviour in ch. **24,** and how should this be expressed in our relationships with other people?

5. What warnings and examples can we draw from the behaviour of Nabal and Abigail (ch. **25**)?

6. Is the gain from temporary expediency ever worth the price paid (ch. **27**—see 2 Chron. **19**.2, James **4**.4.)?

7. How far was David's success as a king the outcome of his experiences of suffering in earlier years?
8. How does 1 Samuel illustrate the truth that "God is not mocked; for whatsoever a man soweth, that shall he also reap"?

2 Samuel 1

Long before the Philistines could find Saul's corpse, a keen-eyed human vulture had seen where he had fallen. As soon as the fighting had moved on, he had stripped him of the royal insignia and had headed south. Had he simply contented himself with bringing the news and the insignia to David, he might have been well rewarded, but he made the fatal mistake of thinking that David was a man with a deep dislike for doing his own dirty work.

Many scholars have built card-houses on the difference between the Amalekite's story and that in the previous chapter. They forget that with nineteen men out of twenty his perversion of facts would have reaped a rich dividend. David's question, "Where do you come from?" (13) finds its explanation in the thought of the time. David knew already that he was a foreigner. If he had been simply in transit, his action might have been condoned as committed in ignorance. When he said, "I am the son of a sojourner," he proclaimed himself one who was allowed to stay in the country on condition that he was subject to its laws. If Saul's armour-bearer did not feel justified in killing Saul, how much less an Amalekite! True he did not actually deserve the death penalty, but, if for the sake of gain we say we have broken the law, should we complain if the law has its way with us?

There are too many textual difficulties in David's lament for them to be mentioned, beyond the fact that the conjectural emendation in v. 21 (R.S.V.) is very doubtful. In v. 24 we have an incidental tribute to the qualities of Saul as king. It does not mean that Saul had a roving eye and a lively sense of feminine beauty. Since women were not touched in normal theft and raiding, a family's surplus assets would be turned into gold and silver ornaments worn by them. David means that by his wise rule Saul had created a prosperity which was reflected in the dress and ornaments of the women; the interpretation that booty taken in war is meant is much less likely.

Though Jonathan took first place in David's lament, there are no grounds for thinking that his mention of Saul was not entirely sincere. Saul, the God-chosen king, had virtually every quality that might be desired except submission to God's will. It may well be that in many ways he was a more outstanding man than David, but the latter possessed the virtue the former lacked, and that made all the difference.

2 Samuel 2

Though David asked God whether he should return to Judah and where, we are not told that he asked whether he should accept the throne of Judah. We cannot know what God's answer would have been, but David's action (see comment on **5.5**) was fraught with fateful consequences.

The message to Jabesh-gilead (5—7) was more than well-earned praise. Official messengers normally knew the message they carried. On their way they will repeatedly have been asked about their mission and message and have repeated it. This both made the fact of David's kingship quickly known and carried the hint that he would not turn down a request to be king of Israel as well.

Ish-bosheth raises many problems—for his name see note on 1 Sam. **14.49**. Apparently he was not at the battle of Mt. Gilboa; neither wife nor child of his is mentioned, and he was quite unable to maintain his dignity against Abner, even when he spoke treason (**3.6**—11). There are only two possibilities which might meet these facts. He could have been a mere lad, but this is contradicted by v. 10 and his place among Saul's sons in 1 Sam. **14.49**. Or he could have been mentally retarded, or a cripple, or in some other way unsuited for kingship. This would explain the discrepancy between his two years' reign (10) and David's seven-and-a-half (11). It will have taken Abner five years to force him gradually on a reluctant Israel, the names in v. 9 showing the stages: "Ashurites" were almost certainly Asherites—*i.e.*, Galilee.

The two kingdoms were at peace until, with Benjamin accepting Ish-bosheth, they had a common frontier. A chance meeting of contingents at the frontier town of Gibeon (12,13) led to the proposal for a little "sport" from Abner (14). Twelve young men—*i.e.*, without wives and children—were chosen on each side. Had one side or the other won, had there been even one to outlive the others for a few minutes and so claim victory, honour would have been satisfied. But faced by a complete draw (16) a general fight was unavoidable. Joab's veterans won a complete victory, but his brother Asahel was killed by Abner, and he was not the man to forget.

It is unlikely that either kingdom wanted to break or win territory from the other, but bloodshed created blood feuds, and so more bloodshed, with the North regularly getting the worst of it. Gradually Abner began to show the cloven hoof (6). Clearly he had put in Ish-bosheth so that later he might quietly slip into his place. The harem of the dead king became the property of his successor. By taking Rizpah (7) Abner was making his first step towards claiming the throne. When Ish-bosheth did not take it lying down, Abner saw that his plans would not go through smoothly; he decided that he had more to gain from being second to David than to Ish-bosheth. One can hardly call it treachery; it was too open for that (9).

For "Michal" (13) see comment on 1 Sam. 25.44. By her return David became after Mephibosheth, who was virtually debarred by his lameness, the leading claimant to the throne of Israel once it was vacated by Ish-bosheth, who might have been glad to abdicate. It is strange that the oracle of v. 18 was not mentioned earlier; it could hardly have been invented by Abner.

There is no reason for suspecting Abner of treachery against David, and it is unlikely that Joab really suspected him (25); he was preparing for his own treachery. "I am this day weak" (39): in the Semitic world the custom of the blood feud was of such antiquity that even the law of Moses did not try to abolish it; it only alleviated it; cf. notes on Josh. 20. Here it is not even suggested that Joab did anything wrong in avenging himself in Hebron. Plainly in the period of the Judges the very existence of cities of refuge had been virtually forgotten. David knew that the blood feud ate at the roots of true justice and government. He was also aware that the death of Asahel was more an excuse than a reason for the murder of Abner. Joab knew that if David made an agreement with Abner, he would take second place after David. But if he was called to account for murder, he could appeal to the "divine right" of the blood feud. It is not until 14.11 that we find David willing to grasp the nettle.

2 Samuel 4.1—5.5

The vultures of the past began to gather round Ish-bosheth. Saul in his efforts to eliminate the descendants of the old Gibeonite league (Josh. 9) tried plain murder (21.1,2). In the case of Beeroth the inhabitants thought it best to move (2,3). The most likely interpretation of this story is that Rimmon was able to hide his identity and continue in Beeroth. His sons had been waiting for their chance for vengeance. This, by all the standards of the time, they would have been entitled to, provided they had not entered Ish-bosheth's service. The freely taken oath of loyalty bound them to him.

Poor Ish-bosheth! He could not even afford a man as porter, and the woman had to combine the post of doorkeeper with kitchen chores. The very different readings in A.V. (K.J.V.) and R.S.V. of v. 6 have essentially the same consonantal text in Hebrew. It is charitable to suppose that in bringing Ish-bosheth's head to David the brothers were not looking for any reward, except, probably, of having a place among his retainers. Their conception of the nature of revenge made them think that David would share it.

If David had been asked on what authority he had had the brothers, or for that matter the Amalekite, killed, he would doubtless have answered that there were some offences so heinous that every man of good will, who had the ability, should deal with them. The modern paraphernalia of law and order has been so developed that it is rare for the private individual to play much part in ensuring justice. This has led to a wide diminution of a sense of moral reprobation towards the more reprehensible law-breaker. It is considered narrow-mindedness if one does not want socially to welcome the drunken driver who has killed, or the adulterer. There is something genuinely refreshing in David's spontaneous outburst of righteous anger.

Mephibosheth (in 1 Chron. 8.34, 9.40, "Meribbaal"—note the long genealogy of his descendants; Jonathan's loyalty was rewarded in this way) was, next to Ish-bosheth, the one real descendant of Saul left. So the writer interrupted the story in 4.4 to tell us of him, and so mitigate in measure the grim story of Ish-bosheth's end.

"He reigned over all Israel and Judah" (5.5): the policy of being made king of Judah first (2.4) was beginning to bear fruit, for it was no longer a single kingdom. Judah and Israel were now separate kingdoms sharing one king.

2 Samuel 5.6–25

The Philistines, having apparently given up hope of a complete conquest of the hill-land of Israel, were not concerned about the existence of two weak and warring kingdoms, the more so as David was presumed friendly in spite of the slur on his honour (1 Sam. 29.4). The union of the kingdoms, however, spelt danger for them, and they attacked at once. That both attacks were directed towards the valley of Rephaim (18,22) suggests that their policy was to split the two kingdoms before David could effectually amalgamate them. A comparison of v. 17 with 23.13—17 suggests that the latter incident is from this period, and that the struggle was longer and fiercer than the bare account of victory suggests. Notice, especially, that under apparently identical circumstances God's guidance varied (19,23). 1 Chron. 14.12 explains the ambiguous v. 21.

The above assumed that vs. 17—25 preceded vs. 6—10 in time (that they do vs. 11—16 is obvious). This is *a priori* probable and is confirmed by "went down to the stronghold" (17). One never "goes down" to Jerusalem in the Bible; David would not have abandoned the strongest point in Central Palestine if he had just captured it. The inversion of order is intended to stress the position of Jerusalem in David's plans. He had intended its capture as his first act of statesmanship.

Benjamin, by failing to capture Jerusalem, had lost all claims to it. Because David captured it, not with the help of the national militia, but by his own personal retainers ("his men", 6), the city became his property. This made it the more suitable as a capital, for it was not attached to any tribe. The translation of v. 8 is sheer guesswork, the Hebrew text being clearly corrupt. The usual explanation, that the city was captured by Joab's climbing up the shaft connecting the city with its water supply (1 Chron. 11.6), is probable, though not certain.

The mention of a palace and an increasing family is an oriental way of stressing David's security. Saul, as archaeology has shown, never found time for building himself a proper palace; he was too involved in constant fighting for such a peace-time occupation.

In v. 20 "Baal" in *Baal-perazim* obviously means "Jehovah"; also "Eliada" (16) is "Beeliada" in 1 Chron. 14.7. It was not until the end of David's reign that this use of Baal as a title for Jehovah officially vanished.

2 Samuel 6

The moving of the ark to Jerusalem was not merely an act of piety, or even a step towards making Jerusalem the religious as well as the civil centre of the people. It was even more David's affirmation of a return to the ideals of the pre-monarchic tribal union, which had centred above all about the ark.

When the Philistines returned the ark on a new, cow-drawn cart (1 Sam. 6.7), they were doing the best they could, short of sending for some Israelite priests to carry it back, so God had accepted their action. Failure to realize His condescension made some think that He had accepted this as a superior method, and so, although it was well known that the ark should be carried by the priests (13), it was assumed that the Philistine method should be followed. Whenever we think that we know better than God's revelation, we are apt to run into serious trouble.

"Baale-judah" (2) is "Baalah" (1 Chron. 13.6)—i.e., Kiriath-jearim. David, ignoring the real reason for Uzzah's death, assumed that Jehovah objected to the ark's being moved and so left it in the house of Obed-edom to see what would happen. When he heard that the ark had brought blessing with it (12), he decided that the removal was not the cause of Uzzah's death and decided to try again. When the first six paces were safely past, David in his intense relief brought a sacrifice (13).

In the Near East until recently it was normal for someone wishing to show special honour to one going in procession to dance before him scantily dressed. His own self-humiliation by scanty dress and wild dancing exalted the one being honoured—so it was with David. His wearing of "a linen ephod" (14) was hardly a claim to priestly or Levitical status, but rather an indication that he was engaged in a sacred ritual.

What are we to say of Michal (16—23)? She had been sorely tried, and we are given no indication of her feelings towards Palti, or Palti-el (1 Sam. 25.44, 2 Sam. 3.15). But the very harshness of David's answer leads us deeper. Michal had been brought up as a king's daughter, and David as a poor farmer's son. Michal had come to respect appearances, and David knew that before God they were meaningless (1 Sam. 16.7). In despising David she was rejecting God's standards.

Is this something we do, without realizing it?

2 Samuel 7

For the writer, David's wars (8) were incidental, and so he handled the other great policy decision of the reign first; v. 1 clearly refers to a fairly late date in his life. Even a prophet can be carried away by what he considers obviously right. If we immediately warm to a new proposal for our church or for some other Christian interest, it is the more reason for examining it most carefully in prayer.

By Divine law the Israelite altar had to be of earth or unhewn stones (Ex. 20.24)—the bronze altar of the Tabernacle was a frame to be filled with earth—and the sanctuary was a tent. In other words, when Tabernacle and altar moved on, there was nothing to indicate that God had been worshipped there, and so no one spot would permanently be regarded as more holy than another. A temple, especially a magnificent one, would be regarded *literally* as God's house, and its site as peculiarly holy. God permitted the building of a temple for the same reason that He permitted a monarchy. The people had fallen so far spiritually, that they could no longer do without it.

The promise to David, "the Lord will make you a house" (11), could, of course, have been made at any other period in his reign, for it is in no sense a reward for his offer to build a temple. But given just here it is for the hearing ear the reminder that it is men and not buildings that God wants. By his prayer (29) David showed that he realized that any such promise contained a conditional element. "Your throne shall be established for ever" (16): this is a promise with a double fulfilment. Taken as conditional, and using the normal secular understanding of the Hebrew translated "for ever", the nineteen generations of the Davidic monarchy were an ample fulfilment (*cf.* 19). Taken in the light of later promises the passage becomes Messianic, and looks forward to One Who should be the perfect dwellingplace of God on earth.

David knew that the promise was not enough in itself; it had to awaken a certain attitude of mind, and so he prayed for a blessing (29). The lesser knelt (in Hebrew "to bless" is linked with the word for "knees") before the greater, and with empty hands held out, awaited their filling in the giving of the blessing.

2 Samuel 8

David's wars, here recorded in summary fashion, give us the impression of wanton aggression, but where we have additional information the picture changes, and we see that David was no fighter for the love of it.

"After this" (1): the information is extracted from the royal chronicles, and refers to the sequel to 5.17—25. "Methegh-ammah": the older interpretation is "the bridle of the mother city"—*i.e.*, a strong point which was essential to the safety of Gath (*cf.* 1 Chron. 18.1). As the most inland of the Philistine cities Gath had always been the spearhead of their attacks on Israel, so its loss meant that from then on Philistia ceased to be much of a threat. The more usual modern explanation is "David took the leading reins out of the hands of the Philistines"—*i.e.*, Israel, not the Philistines, was now dominant in Palestine.

While the defeat and capture of Moab need not surprise us, the barbarous treatment of its warriors should. Nearly two-thirds of the prisoners were massacred (2), though "one full line" shows that a certain minimum of mercy was shown. Jewish tradition is that the king of Moab had David's parents killed (*cf.* 1 Sam. **22**.3,4), but this may have been invented to explain the cruelty. An attack in the back, like Edom's, during the Syrian campaign is more likely.

For more detail of the war with Syria see **10**.6—19, from which we see it was forced on David. David made himself king of the nearer Syrian territory of Damascus, but was only overlord of the more distant areas. With v. 13, *cf.* title of Psa. **60** and 1 Kings **11**.15,16. Obviously at the height of the struggle with the Syrians Edom attacked him in the rear; the terrible vengeance exacted suggests there was treachery as well. The result of all this fighting was that David became king of Judah and Israel, Edom, Moab, Ammon and Damascus, as well as overlord of the other areas mentioned.

With vs. 15—18 *cf.* the somewhat later list, **20**.23—26. David was in charge of justice (15). Read "Abiathar, the son of Ahimelech" and probably "the son of Ahitub" (17; *cf.* 1 Sam. **22**.11,20, 2 Sam. **20**.25). "Recorder" (16): better "remembrancer"; he had to keep David up to date with business and make his decisions known. "David's sons were priests" (18): "priest" is probably used in its secular sense—*i.e.*, as having immediate access to the royal presence.

Questions for Further Study and Discussion on 2 Samuel chapters 1—8.
1. What does David's lament reveal about his qualities of character (ch. **1**)?
2. In the light of ch. **2** consider the way in which human codes of honour can be taken too far.
3. What does ch. **3** have to teach us about the dangers of compromise, in the light of God's Law? Compare Deut. **17**.17.
4. What is the New Testament answer to the claim that the story of Uzzah (ch. **6**) illustrates a primitive view of a God of wrath of most uncertain temper? (See Heb. **10**.28,29).
5. What are the great themes and the searching questions revealed in David's prayer (ch. **7**)?

2 Samuel 9.1—11.1

From here to 20.22, and then 1 Kings 1,2, we have a history written by someone at the court of David, who was in touch with all that was going on—Abiathar and Ahimaaz, the son of Zadok, are popular guesses. Obviously 9.1 must have happened soon after 5.3. "Servant" (9.2,9)—*i.e.*, slave; there is nothing incongruous in his having slaves also (9.10). David recognized Mephibosheth as Saul's legal heir, and gave him honourable status at court, but in such a way as to keep him under supervision if there was any talk of revolt by supporters of Saul's dynasty.

Evidently Nahash, the old adversary of Saul (1 Sam. 11), had helped David during his flight from Saul (10.2). We cannot explain the wanton light-heartedness of Hanun and his ministers. 10.6 suggests that they had expected David to swallow the insult; a greater could hardly have been devised. Perhaps they thought him preoccupied with the Philistines. That some preoccupation existed is shown in David's sending only part of his forces—"the host of the mighty men" (10.7)—and that only when the Ammonites had hired a large mercenary army. It was so well known that Ammon had only one city of any size—*viz.* Rabbah (11.1)—that the identity of the city in 10.8,14 is not indicated. The threat of the mercenaries removed, Joab returned; David's vengeance could wait.

Hadadezer evidently had his ambitions and recognized in David a dangerous rival. David's immediate reaction (10.17) probably took the Syrians by surprise. The site of "Helam" is uncertain, but it was probably in the Damascus area. "Forty thousand horsemen" (10.18): 1 Chron. 19.18, correctly "forty thousand footmen", *cf.* 8.4,5. That number of "horsemen" would imply well over 10,000 chariots, hardly a possible number. The same verse gives 1,700 chariots; the 1,000 has dropped in *Samuel*, *cf.* 8.4. 8.4,5 shows that the campaign was in two stages and the total footmen were 42,000.

With the return of the proper campaigning season the turn of Ammon had come. David has repeatedly been blamed for staying in Jerusalem. We must first remember 21.15—17, which almost certainly took place earlier; this was the recognition that a king meant more than merely a war leader. Further, the feeling throughout the story, and the only explanation of the Ammonite folly, is that David was preoccupied with some other unspecified difficulty, internal or external. Let us leave judgment to the only One entitled to judge.

David had a summer-room on the palace roof (*cf.* Judg. 3.23), which was the highest point in Jerusalem. Bath-sheba belonged to court circles and she must have known that David might see her. "The daughter of Eliam" (3): if this is the Eliam of 23.34, Bath-sheba was Ahitophel's granddaughter, but the link is never made (see comment on 15.31).

Both David and Bath-sheba seem to have assumed that Uriah would regard the royal attentions to his wife as an honour. So long as the child could theoretically be his, the proprieties had been observed. There seems to have been nothing particularly secret about the affair; Uriah probably had his suspicions and just "would not play ball". The force of v. 11 is probably: "The ark is housed in a tent; the bulk of the people sleep in the fields, because it is harvest time; the army sleeps as best it may." It seems impossible not to see an implied rebuke of David. There is no suggestion that the ark was with the army.

If Joab knew the motive behind David's letter, he was not the man to make any bones about it. He was probably none too sorry to get David down to his own level. David envisaged a clumsy plan for getting Uriah killed (15), Joab improved on it; he was not concerned if others lost their lives, too (16,17). "Jerubbesheth" (21)—*i.e.*, Jerubbaal, or Gideon; Baal has been replaced by *bosheth* (shame), with a change of vowels for euphony (see comment on 1 Sam. 14.49). In the whole foul story David's answer is perhaps the most degrading part (25).

Uriah was one of David's special group of thirty, his mighty men (23.8—39). No disloyalty is recorded of them, but David was disloyal to them. We cannot help asking ourselves how genuine Bath-sheba's lamentations were.

If we read the histories of kings and great men of other nations, we shall find many another such story, though the husband generally saw in time on which side his bread was buttered. Until recently kings were often regarded as above the law, and men applauded their vices so long as they did not hurt the taxpayers' pockets. But God makes no exceptions to the demands of His moral law.

Doubtless Nathan's duties included watching out for cases of injustice which had failed to reach the king's ears. So there will have been nothing in his story to awaken David's suspicions. For us it would, at the worst, have been a case of robbery with violence. David, with a far truer understanding of justice, took the revelation of the rich man's character into consideration. Our sentimentalists would object to death penalty (5) *and* fourfold restitution (6). But what good did the death penalty do to the poor man? It is easy so to be occupied with law as to forget that it should be a servant for the achieving of justice.

"You are the man" (7): David had passed sentence of death on himself. Before giving the two main charges, Nathan stressed the enormity of David's action (7,8): God had saved David, made him king, and though he had been one of Saul's retainers, had given him legally all that had been Saul's (there is no suggestion that he had actually married any members of Saul's harem). Surely God would have given him anything else reasonable. The first charge is murder to gain another's wife (9,10); the penalty, the continuance of "the sword" in his house. The second charge is adultery (11,12); the penalty, the open degrading of his wives.

David confessed his sin frankly, and Nathan pronounced the remission of the death penalty, but brought forward a new charge (14). The R.S.V. text is based on the probably correct supposition that "enemies of" was introduced by the scribes for reverential reasons. God exacts a penalty for the way He has been despised—*i.e.*, the death of his son. The first penalty, that for murder, can be seen not merely in the death of Amnon, Absalom, and Adonijah, but also in the bloodshed under Athaliah (2 Kings 11.1) and various later assassinations. The second penalty, that for adultery, was mitigated but not abolished (16.21,22).

David's reaction when his son sickened and died (15—23) was a public acknowledgement of God's justice; mourning for him could have been interpreted as dissatisfaction with God's action. God's love to Solomon was shown above all in his living, which in turn was a sign of grace to the forgiven father. The name Jedidiah is not found elsewhere.

Rabbah lies on a hill above the Jabbok. "The royal city" or "the city of waters" controlled the access to the water supply. Its capture meant that Rabbah could not long resist. David put the Ammonites to forced labour.

2 Samuel 13.1–36

Amnon's passion for Tamar can on the one hand be understood. Many wives, many children, the boys separated from the girls after five or six; there would not be the sense of belonging together that exists in a normal family. On the other hand, as his sudden revulsion showed (15), there was something pathological in it. Like the evil spirit that had come on Saul, God's hand was behind it, as is further shown by David's nephew's part in precipitating the tragedy (3—5). It is usually maintained that v. 13 shows that marriage between half-brother and sister, though forbidden by the law, was still practised. More likely Tamar was desperately clutching at straws to save herself.

"David was very angry" (21): David is attacked on all sides for his softness to his sons—it is hardly fair to apply 1 Kings 1.6 to them all—but such charges show lack of psychological understanding. At the time crimes committed within the family, like Amnon's, were the sole concern of the family and above all of its head. So David was free to punish as he wished. But how was he, who saw the punishment for his own sin being worked out before his eyes, to punish the guilty?

How did Jonadab know (32) that Amnon only had been killed? For that matter, how did Absalom guess at once (20) that Amnon was the cause of Tamar's grief? Was it a mere coincidence that in removing the man who had wronged his sister, Absalom also made himself heir-presumptive to the throne? Perhaps Absalom had planted Jonadab in Amnon's household to ruin him. If Tamar was involved in his ruin, what of it if Absalom became king? Otherwise it is hard to account for his self-control, which gave Amnon no positive reason for suspecting his hostility (22); no one seems to have suspected his motive even when he specially stressed his invitation to Amnon. The drunkenness of the feast gave Absalom more time to get away.

In 1 Kings 1.17 there is a reference to David's oath to Bath-sheba that Solomon should succeed him. It will have been a private one, but suspicion as to its existence must have been rife. There was not yet an established custom that the eldest son should succeed, but it will have been regarded by most as natural. Ambitious Absalom will have felt compelled to establish his position while Solomon was still young.

2 Samuel 13.37—14.27

Geshur was independent, but its king probably paid tribute. Had David insisted, Talmai would probably have had to hand over

Absalom, his daughter's son. David had probably no wish to insist and was secretly pleased that he was spared dealing with Absalom.

Joab seems to have been a single-minded patriot, whose loyalty to David was bound up with his conviction that the greatness of Israel depended on him. If he obviously thought that the greatness of Israel meant also the greatness of Joab, that was a blind spot that many such men have shared. At this point (1) he was moved with affection neither for David nor Absalom, but by the wish to settle the question of the succession. After some hints to David (cf. 19), he decided to appeal to David's sense of justice.

The widow's story was not uncommon (4—11). One son of a widow accidentally killed the other and was evidently hidden by her. The heads of the family, with whom authority lay, insisted on justice and blood for blood. The widow's plea was that this involved greater injustice for her. She was in fact asking the king to declare that royal justice stood higher than family justice and the bloodfeud. Having extracted an oath from David (11), she charged him with wrong in overruling the law for her but not in the far more important case of Absalom, where the welfare of the land as a whole was at stake (12—14). She ended (15—17) by suggesting that it was her own trouble that had brought her to the king, and that the other matter had just slipped out.

David saw through this at once, and gave Joab permission to have Absalom back, but would not let him come to court. This was not imperfect forgiveness but the clear statement that he would not recognize him as successor. David did not allow affection to blind him to the realities of Absalom's character.

The Semites suffered from the same delusion as the Greeks, and others since. Beauty of heart and body, or ugliness of heart and body, do not necessarily go together. Absalom's perfect physical beauty prevented men's seeing his selfishness and worthlessness. His hair was probably worn in many plaits as is the custom with many Bedouin men today. There is no contradiction between v. 27 and 18.18. His sons probably died young.

2 Samuel 14.28—15.29

With one like Absalom compromises are useless. He found that as long as he was debarred from court he was no nearer his ambition (14.32). Joab soon realized that he had judged wrongly, but he had a tiger by the tail (29,30). David had to recognize that the compromise would not work (33).

David is blamed for not acting, when Absalom adopted royal pomp, but at the time it was not royal pomp in Israel, it was only showing off. Behind the story as it develops there is a cool master mind. It can hardly have been Absalom's; he does not create that impression. It could have been Jonadab's, but he is not mentioned again; the traditional identification with Ahitophel is probably correct. Note that in the rest of this story the northern and southern kingdoms are carefully identified as Israel and Judah.

Absalom tried to win the North, Israel (2,6). Why the average person believed him is a mystery. Obviously there were delays, and the disappointed litigant will always believe that the judge has been less than fair. But if the woman from Tekoa could reach the royal presence and have a full hearing it suggests that Absalom was doing some hard lying.

He had his eyes on the North, so he went south to Hebron to be crowned! The two hundred Jerusalem guests (11) were intended to confuse David, who could not know who was loyal to him. That is why he abandoned Jerusalem (14). When treachery is abroad, the open country among those one can trust is better than the doubtful security of walls. He was accompanied by his retainers, mighty men and mercenaries. "And Ittai the Gittite" has dropped out in v. 18 before "and all the six hundred Gittites". David made a distinction between Ittai and the other mercenaries. The latter had been long enough in his service to owe him loyalty, the former had not had time really to owe him anything.

David was not unwilling to fight; Absalom was too bad a man to let him tamely become king. But he was not willing to let the super-stitious say that he had triumphed by forcing God to take his side, so he sent the priests back, but enrolled them in his schemes.

If it is asked why Israel so easily rejected David, and Judah re-mained passive, the answer is that, once danger is past, it comes naturally to very many to resent true greatness. We prefer to celebrate it in retrospect.

2 Samuel 15.30—16.19

"Ahitophel is among the conspirators" (31): the opinion is often met that Ahitophel was acting in revenge for the dishonour done him through his granddaughter (see note on 11.3). Such a theory gives him a great-grandson of twelve, if not more. Would he at that age have offered to lead a risky and strenuous night attack (17.1)? Normally for an oriental to see a daughter or granddaughter in the royal harem was welcomed, for it meant a sure road to advancement. The theory also assumes that he wanted to destroy his granddaughter, for that would have been the sure result of Absalom's victory.

Hushai (for "Archite", see Josh. **16.**2) was "David's friend" (37); this was an appointment of extreme confidence at court. "You will be a burden to me" (33) shows that he was elderly.

It is difficult to know what to think of Ziba. He must have had a genuine loyalty to David, for Mephibosheth would lose his favoured position once Absalom triumphed, and Ziba might have to pay heavily, if it was known that he had helped David. That he was exaggerating is certain (3), but it is possible that it was not all lies. We need not doubt the truth of Mephibosheth's words in **19.**26,27, and yet the cripple may have had harmless daydreams of what he might have been, which in the moment of crisis may have made him dither long enough for Ziba to go off without him. His presence with David might have kept men like Shimei quiet. The gift to Ziba (4) was of very considerable value and presumably made him a free man.

Shimei was a distant relation of Saul's. He probably believed the worst rumours about the deaths of Abner and Ish-bosheth, and placed the worst construction on **21.**1—9. David's restraint came from his recognizing that though Shimei's curses were groundless, he could have cursed him for the sins he had committed. In picturing David's withdrawal, we should not forget that apart from the soldiers there were many women and children. David was not the only one to bring his family with him.

Even Absalom was somewhat shocked by the fulsomeness of Hushai's greeting. The complete cynicism of his answer (18) won Absalom's confidence, for he thought he had found a man of his own character.

2 Samuel 16.20—17.29

"Go in to your father's concubines" (**16.**21): though the king's son took over his father's harem as part of his property, there is no evidence that, in Israel, he had any sexual relations with them. That would have been incest. Ahitophel's advice showed not merely fiendish hatred of David, but virtually caused Absalom to disown David and all he stood for. Absalom was a simple character, driven by ambition, but behind him were some who wanted to change the whole basis of the Israelite state.

Hushai triumphed over Ahitophel because he understood Absalom better. If we compare Ahitophel's "Let me choose . . . and I will" (1) with Hushai's "You go to battle in person" (11), the difference is obvious. At the same time there was more in Hushai's advice than is often recognized. To control an army of twelve thousand in a night attack over the very difficult and broken ground between Jerusalem and the Jordan was a major task. If it succeeded, it would be fatal to David, but the wiser of Absalom's counsellors could see the possibility and result of failure. Ahitophel, in his bitter disloyalty, discounted the loyalty of those with David.

"Ahitophel hanged himself" (17.23): if we could know with certainty the cause of his suicide, we should understand the hidden forces behind the rebellion much better. Here are two considerations: (a) Ahitophel had been the real power behind Absalom's plotting, and he could have expected to be the power behind the scenes after his triumph. But now he had taken the bit between his teeth and had been carried away by crude flattery (17.11—13). There was no certain future for Ahitophel. (b) He had a premonition of coming defeat. He had been carried on unerringly by a daemonic force. It had been checked, and he knew the end had come.

David's reception at Mahanaim, Ish-bosheth's former capital, was warmer than he could have dared to expect. "Shobi" (27) was Hanun's brother (10.1). David had evidently appointed him regent in Ammon, and he reaped the gratitude of loyalty. "Machir" had looked after Mephibosheth (9.4), and now he repaid David's kindness. "Barzillai" will have been the leading personality of Gilead.

2 Samuel 18.1—19.8

The frequent suggestion that David was showing distrust or resentment by putting Joab over only a third of the army (18.2) is baseless. In fact the ground between Mahanaim and the Jordan is so broken that no fully co-ordinated battle front was to be expected. For "the forest of Ephraim" cf. Judg. 12.4. The battle can never have been started on such broken ground. Though Absalom had nominated Amasa as general (17.25), it is doubtful if he was even on the battle-field, where Absalom was in personal command. David's experienced generals manœuvred him in his inexperience into drawing up his army with the broken ground behind him. The moment he began to retreat his lines were irreparably broken, and no further organized resistance was possible.

Whether Absalom could have been caught by his hair in the traditional way is doubtful. The Bible says it was his head, not his hair, that was caught. The runaway mule will have driven his head with such force into a fork of the branches as to stun him and leave him hanging. Joab's complete ruthlessness was common property (13), but here he judged rightly that Absalom had to die.

Joab's messenger was not "Cushi" but a "Cushite" (21)—*i.e.*, a Negro slave. Joab could not anticipate how David might receive the news; he might in his anguish even kill its bringer. Ahimaaz, on the other hand, foresaw the brutality with which the slave would announce Absalom's death, and he wished to spare David a little. Joab probably misjudged his speed and better knowledge of the ground (23) when he allowed him to run also. By his strong hint (29) Ahimaaz must have prepared David for the Negro's brutally triumphant proclamation.

Let us judge Absalom as we will and David's treatment of him as we may, we have no right to condemn David in the hour of his overwhelming grief. "Would I had died instead of you" (33) is the brokenhearted confession of a man who knew that he had killed his son by his sin. However much Absalom contributed to it; however much evil men stood behind him and pushed him on; quite literally he had died because David had murdered Uriah. Joab clearly had no understanding for the deeper causes of his grief (19.5,6).

2 Samuel 19.9–43

David behaved about Absalom much as he had about his baby boy (12.20). He could not call the dead back, but he could start mending the broken pieces. He had to walk warily and not rush things. Israel had deposed him (note how their language in v. 9 bore out the premonitions of Josh. 22.24) and Judah was sulking, not very sure what to do.

With a little judicious prompting the latter responded enthusiastically (11—15), perhaps even too much so. Interestingly, Benjamin, at least in part, foreshadowed what would happen under Rehoboam, when they took the side of Judah. Their brief experience under Absalom had convinced all but the fanatics among them that the old days of Benjaminite grandeur under Saul had gone for ever. We cannot tell whether Shimei had had a change of heart, or whether he acted in sheer policy (16,17). David would have been glad to punish him, but had he done so, there were thousands of others who would have feared his wrath, and in fear resisted. Ziba remains an enigma (17); we still do not know whether it is love for David that is driving him, or the fear that certain lies might be coming home to roost.

There is a harshness about David's reply to Mephibosheth (29) that repels us. Yet the fact remained that Ziba had helped David when it mattered most, while Mephibosheth sat helplessly and uselessly in Jerusalem. David had bigger tasks facing him than getting to the bottom of the story. History tells us no more of Chimham (37), but Jeremiah 41.17 suggests that David gave him a property near Bethlehem out of his private estate.

Judah's action had a tragi-comic result. The news of Judah's action spread quickly, and by the time David was ready to cross the Jordan representatives of half Israel were waiting for him (40). On the way up to Jerusalem a fully representative delegation had come to meet him. They were annoyed, for they seemed to think that their talk had created a sort of option on David, until they made up their mind. To make matters worse, Judah had virtually kidnapped David—*i.e.*, the fords of Jordan at Gilgal were on Israelite territory, but Judah had ignored this. We are not told what was said in the slanging match that followed, but tempers ran high. David had been a little too clever.

2 Samuel 20

Where tempers run high, people act without thinking. Sheba, a Benjaminite, evidently nursed the tribal grudge against David. His call to the delegation to abandon David had startling results (2). David had to leave the matter until he could establish himself in Jerusalem (2,3). Those who had come to meet him at the Jordan were only representative delegations, so he sent Amasa, the new commander-in-chief (19.13), to raise the Judean militia at top speed. Though Amasa was used to depose Joab, the choice was wise, because Amasa had been Absalom's commander-in-chief (17.25). Amasa had not the organizational skill to accomplish the task in the time set, so David had to send off his regulars under Abishai (7); Joab went as one of the mighty men.

Amasa, hearing what was afoot, rushed north with all the men he had gathered and reached Gibeon first (8). In killing Absalom Joab had killed for the state and the dynasty; now he murdered for the good of Joab himself. He had so arranged his sword, that as he started to embrace Amasa for the kiss of peace, it dropped into his free hand. As soon as they did not have Amasa's corpse to trouble them, the militia, accustomed to Joab's leadership, followed him. So Joab calmly slipped back into the position of general.

It was soon obvious that Sheba's revolt was an anti-climax. As soon as his companions recovered from the angry words, they slipped away, and the only ones to join him were his own clansmen (14). As he marched north the cities shut their gates to him until he found refuge with his small band of men in the far north at Abel-beth-maachah.

Why its citizens received him, we do not know, but as soon as they saw that Joab was in earnest, they called for a parley (16). That it was conducted by a woman suggests that the contingent Abel had sent to Absalom's army had not yet returned. As soon as the townsmen realized what was really involved, that was the end of Sheba (22) and of the fighting.

For vs. 23—26 *cf*. **8**.16—18. This is slightly later, for now we meet "Adoram in charge of the forced labour" (*cf*. 1 Kings **4**.6; **12**.18); though this was a widely used form of labour in lieu of taxes, it was deeply resented. Sheva is a variant spelling of Seraiah (**8**.17; *cf*. 1 Kings **4**.3); he was a foreigner, whose name did not lend itself to Hebrew spelling. "Ira the Jairite" will probably have been a private secretary (*cf*. **8**.17,18).

2 Samuel 21

We now begin the appendix and read of various important matters which had no obvious place in the earlier chapters.

Vs. 1—14 deal with a legacy of sacrilegious murder David inherited from Saul. Continual famine caused by inadequate rain convinced David that there must be unexpiated sin over the land; a divine oracle declared that it was the result of Saul's breaking the oath sworn in the days of Joshua (Josh. **9**.15) to the members of the Gibeonite league (see comment on **4**.2,3). The Gibeonites, when summoned to David's presence, indicated that they wanted an expiation that they as non-citizens were not entitled to ask (4). When assured they could ask freely, they demanded the death of seven of Saul's sons, indicating that a money ransom would not be accepted. It is often suggested by liberal scholars that the whole matter was too opportune for David not to have been rigged, but it is doubtful whether any of those hanged could ever have made a serious bid for the throne. The maternal devotion of Rizpah (10) could have lasted from April to October, but there may have been a few late showers about the end of April. The Gibeonites probably had primitive ideas about God, so the leaving of the bodies on the gallows was to let God see that punishment had been inflicted. We shrink from a story like this, but no one can break a solemn oath with impunity. God's punishments come in the way that those that suffer them understand best.

The stories of David's battles began with his killing of Goliath; they end with his nearly being killed by another giant (15—17). The incident must have been near the end of the struggle with the Philistines, when David had consolidated his position as king of the two countries. This leads to the mention of the death of some other giants. There can be little doubt that 1 Chron. 20.5 contains the correct version of v. 19. "Jaareoregim" must be read as Jair. With this change the differences are small in Hebrew. There are those that would read "and Elhanan the son of Jesse . . ." claiming that Elhanan was the personal, David the throne-name of the killer of Goliath. This is possible, but highly improbable.

2 Samuel 22.1—23.7

In this section David's work as a psalmist is summed up and typified by two psalms. The former (22.2—51) is the same as Psalm 18. A comparison between the two versions would be profitable, for it would show that both have been copied with care, but for all that minor changes have slipped in. This psalm was chosen by the editor of *Samuel* because it is a commemoration of God's care and protection generally and not in one particular incident in his life. The latter is "the last words of David" (23.1—7). It was not included in the Psalter, for it is not suited to public worship in spite of its great beauty. "Last words" need not be understood as meaning that he spoke them on his death bed. In the evening of his life, as death drew near, he summed up his experiences of God and of life.

David's experience of God was primarily as "Saviour"—*i.e.*, Giver of victory (22.2—4). He had repeatedly found himself on the verge of death, but God had always heard him (5—7). It is only the general context that shows that the dangers of war are intended here; it would have been equally true of other dangers. In the elaborate language in which he describes God coming to his aid (8—16) David implies that He used all the resources of Nature in helping him. He then describes his deliverance (17—20). This was due not merely to grace, but because he sought to walk according to His will (21—25), and above all because he was humble (26—31). He sings of the grace and help of God (32—43) by which he had become potentially the ruler of the world (44—51). Had God willed that he should extend his campaigns, he would have been equally successful.

Because his Last Words might be heard beyond Israel, David introduces himself (23.1) and claims inspiration (2,3a). He then uses two pictures of the righteous ruler (3b—5). The righteous king dispensing justice is like the sun rising on a clear morning before things are hidden by haze and dust. Things are seen as they really are with all the sophistries and lies of men defeated. Then he is the refresher of men as he has been refreshed by God. The righteousness continues with his descendants (5). Finally, from bitter experience, he gives a picture of the character, danger, and worthlessness of evil men (6,7).

2 Samuel 23.8—24.25

David instituted an order of thirty mighty men, perhaps in Ziklag, to act as his bodyguard. If there are thirty-seven here (39), and another sixteen in 1 Chron. **11**, it is because some members were promoted to higher office and some died, and the vacancies were filled. *Samuel* stops at Uriah as a reminder of David's unfaithfulness to the faithful. The three (8—12) are included in the thirty, as are Abishai (18,19) and Benaiah (20—23). To obtain the thirty-seven names we must add Joab. He is implied but omitted because his crimes made him unworthy of his place.

Ch. 24 stands in its present position not for chronological reasons but because it looks forward to *Kings* and the building of the Temple, for which it is a direct preparation. "Again" (1) may refer back to 21.1—14. The reason for God's anger is not even hinted at. At the time the wrongness of the census, felt even by a man like Joab (3), was so obvious that the writer has not explained why. It is sometimes suggested that it was because the half-shekel tax was not paid (Exod. 30.11—16). For all we know, it may have been, but Joab's language implies an objection to the census as such, not to the neglect of an important ritual detail. The same applies to David's confession of guilt (10). It is likely that David was contemplating a change in the military organization, which would need a knowledge of the man-power at his disposal (*cf.* 9).

The punishment, by which David lost seventy thousand men (15), would be an appropriate one, if such was his fault. If it is objected that it is unfair on those who died, the answer may lie in the unexplained anger of v. 1. David showed his wisdom in letting the punishment be inflicted entirely by God (14).

The variety in the spelling of Araunah's name (*cf.* 1 Chron. **21.15**) is probably because it was a Hittite name (*cf.* Ezek. **16.3**), hard to fit into Hebrew. It may be that, in contrast with Gen. **23.11**, Araunah was genuinely giving the site to David (22,23) as his contribution to the stopping of the plague. But this was David's offering for David's sin, and so it had to cost David.

Thought: What you have gained from these three months' studies depends on how much time and effort you gave.

Questions for Further Study and Discussion on 2 Samuel chapters 9—24.

1. In ch. **11** trace the links in the chain of temptation and sin (vs. 2—4,8,13,15).
2. Can you find material in verses like **13.26,36,** and **39** for drawing a comparison and a contrast between David's love for his sinful sons and God's love for His sinful family? Can you trace New Testament parallels to David's thought in **16.10** that God can bring good out of evil? How effective is this in countering the desire for revenge?
3. What philosophy of history can we see in **17.14**?
4. How may we fall into the trap of giving the impression that we have greater "shares" in Jesus Christ than anyone else (**19.43**)?
5. Study **22.2,3** in the light of Luther's words, "The whole of religion lies in the personal pronouns."
6. How many attributes of God can you find in **22.8—20**?

© 1966 Scripture Union
First Published 1966
Reprinted 1966

Published in Daily Bible Commentary Vol. 1, 1977
Reprinted 1977
First published in this edition 1978

ISBN 0 85421 633 2

Printed and bound in Great Britain by
McCorquodale (Newton) Ltd, Newton-le-Willows